+++++++++++++++++++++++++++++++++++++++++

# THE GOSPEL OF ST JOHN
## *The Story of the Son of God*

+++++++++++++++++++++++++++++++++++++++++++++++++++++++++++++++++++++++++++++++++++++

INTRODUCED AND EDITED BY JOHN DRANE
FOREWORD BY PIERS PAUL READ

*St. Martin's Griffin*
*New York*

ISBN 0-312-22209-2 cloth
ISBN 0-312-22077-4 paperback

Library of Congress Cataloging-in-Publication Data
is available from the Library of Congress.


First published in Great Britain by Lion Publishing plc, 1997.
First St. Martin's Griffin edition: June 1999
10 9 8 7 6 5 4 3 2 1

# Contents

Acknowledgments    6

Foreword    7

## Introduction    9

John and the Synoptic Gospels    9

The Background of John in Judaism    11

Archaeological Discoveries    12

The Author and Date of Writing    13

The Purpose and Structure of John    15

## The Gospel of St John in Literature    19

Themes and Images    20

Major Characters    42

## The Gospel of St John    91

Part One: The Light Revealed    95

Part Two: The Darkness Defeated    130

Index of Primary Sources    157

# ACKNOWLEDGMENTS

The text of 'The Gospel of St John in Literature' has been selected from
*A Dictionary of Biblical Tradition in English Literature*, edited by David Lyle
Jeffrey, copyright © 1992 by permission of Wm B. Eerdmans Publishing Co.

The unabridged text of The Gospel of St John has been taken from the *New
Jerusalem Bible* copyright © 1985 by permission of Darton, Longman and
Todd Ltd and Doubleday and Company Inc.

Margaret Avison, 'The Circuit', has been reproduced from *Sunblue* (1978),
published by Oxford University Press, Canada.

# Foreword

The Gospel of St John presents a paradox. On the one hand it is the most composed and reflective of the four gospels, and so lacks the simplicity and immediacy of the other three. On the other, it is the gospel that was clearly written by someone who not only knew Jesus but witnessed the events he describes. The most recent scholarship accepts that the author was 'a primary source', almost certainly the same John described in the gospel as 'the disciple whom Jesus loved', the man to whom he entrusted his mother at the foot of the cross.

Yet this gospel is much more than mere reportage. The author may have witnessed the life, death and resurrection of Jesus, but he has had a lifetime to ponder over what he had heard and what he had seen. We sense that the Holy Spirit has given St John a greater understanding of the mystery of Jesus than we find in the other three Evangelists. It is he who realizes, in the majestic words of the opening of the first chapter, that Jesus was 'the Word made flesh'.

Two things in particular strike me about this gospel, both of which tend to be overlooked today. The first is the necessity of faith in Jesus as the only Son of God. Jesus and the Father are one. 'If you know me, you know my Father too… To have seen me is to have seen the Father…' (John 14:6–7, 9). He alone is our salvation. 'I am the resurrection. If anyone believes in me, even though he dies he will live, and whoever lives and believes in me will never die' (John 11:25–26).

The second is Jesus' unambiguous words about the Eucharist in chapter 6: 'I am the bread of life… I tell you most solemnly, if you do not eat the flesh of the Son of Man and drink his blood, you will not have life in you.' St John does not conceal the alienating effect of this audacious statement on Jesus' audience in 1st-century Palestine. 'After hearing it, many of his followers said, "This is intolerable language. How could anyone accept it?" After this, many of his disciples left him and stopped going with him' (John 6:45, 52, 60).

It was the same with Jesus' claim to be the Son of God. It provoked outrage. 'He is possessed, he is raving; why bother to listen to him?' (John 10:20). Even among those who believed some were too frightened of public opinion to admit it. 'They put honour from men before the honour that comes from God.'

If we recognize the scepticism of the modern world in these reactions to Jesus, we can equally respond with faith to the unique qualities of the extraordinary man portrayed by St John – his compassion, his authority and his power over death. The cry 'Lazarus, come forth' (John 12:43) resounds down the ages, and will be heard by all who can say with Lazarus' sister Martha: 'Yes, Lord, I believe that you are the Christ, the Son of God' (John 11:27).

*Piers Paul Read*

# INTRODUCTION

There was a time, fifty or sixty years ago, when biblical scholars regarded the Gospel of John as a 2nd-century theological interpretation of the life of Jesus using the language and thought-forms of Hellenistic philosophy. They thought of it as a kind of extended sermon, with no real connection with reliable traditions about Jesus as he actually lived and taught.

Recent developments, however, have shattered this picture of John's Gospel once and for all. Many competent scholars are now prepared to regard it as an early, independent source of knowledge about Jesus' life and teaching, and of equal value with the synoptic gospels. We can trace three main reasons for this radical change of opinion: the gospels of Matthew, Mark and Luke, commonly called the Synoptics.

## John and the Synoptic Gospels

Sixty years ago it was widely assumed that the author of John's Gospel knew the synoptic gospels. The reason for this was the number of stories common to both. (The story of how Jesus fed the 5,000 and the story of his anointing at Bethany are examples.) It was therefore supposed that John was writing a kind of 'theological' interpretation of the 'factual' stories of the synoptic gospels. This inevitably led to the conclusion that the fourth gospel must be later in date and inferior in quality to the synoptic gospels.

This assumption has, however, been questioned at two points. First of all, it is now widely recognized that it is not possible to set the 'history' of the Synoptics over against the 'theology' of John. The synoptic writers were themselves theologians. They did not write their gospels for purely biographical reasons, but because they had a message for their readers. Secondly, it has also been demonstrated that the fourth gospel is not really dependent on the other three, and

9

indeed its author may well have written his work without any knowledge of the writings of the other evangelists.

Closer examination of these stories found in all four gospels shows that though there are similarities, there are also a number of differences in John's account, and these differences are not the kind that can easily be explained on theological grounds. John's variations are in fact much easier to understand if we assume that he had access to different reports of the incidents known also to the synoptic writers. When this hypothesis is tested in detail, it can be seen not only that John's account comes from a different source, but also that there are a number of pieces of information in John which can be used to supplement the accounts of the other gospels in such a way that the whole story of Jesus' life and ministry becomes more understandable.

For example, John reports that some of Jesus' disciples had previously been followers of John the Baptist. This helps to explain the exact nature of the Baptist's witness to Jesus in the Synoptics, and especially the emphasis placed there on his role in 'preparing the way of the Lord'. John's account also helps to identify what Jesus was doing between his baptism and the arrest of John the Baptist. The Synoptics report that Jesus began his ministry in Galilee after John's arrest, and this is the only ministry recorded in the synoptic gospels. But Matthew and Luke (Q) report that during his last visit to Jerusalem, Jesus said of its inhabitants, 'How often would I have gathered your children together...' (Matthew 23:37; Luke 13:34) – which suggests Jesus had visited Jerusalem on previous occasions. John reports just such an occasion, right at the beginning of Jesus' ministry, when he worked alongside John the Baptist in Judea before going back to Galilee when John was arrested.

John's Gospel illustrates and supplements the synoptic material at a later point, when it records another visit by Jesus to Jerusalem some six months before his entry on Palm Sunday. John records how Jesus left Galilee and went to Jerusalem for the Feast of Tabernacles (September) and stayed there until the Feast of Dedication (December). Then, because of growing hostility, he returned to the area where John the Baptist had worked, and only made a brief visit to Bethany when he heard that Lazarus had died. A little later, six days before the Passover (April) he returned for his final visit to Jerusalem. This is the only one recorded in any detail in Mark, though the others are perhaps implied by Mark's summary statement: 'he left [Galilee] and went to the region of Judea and beyond the Jordan'.

Many smaller details provided by John's Gospel also help to explain and clarify some points in the synoptic narratives. There is, for example, the feeding of the 5,000. At the end of the story in Mark, Jesus forces his disciples to escape on a boat while he stays behind to dismiss the crowd. John's independent tradition fills in some of the detail, explaining that Jesus took this action because the crowd were eager to kidnap him and make him their king. Similarly, the stories of the Last Supper and of Jesus' trials can be fully understood only in the light of information contained in John's Gospel.

In view of evidence of this sort, it is now coming to be realized that John's Gospel is a source in its own right. The information it contains is independent of that in the synoptic gospels, but at many crucial points John complements the other three.

## The Background of John in Judaism

Early traditions place the origin of this gospel in Ephesus, and so scholars naturally looked for a Hellenistic background, especially in view of the gospel's prologue which explains the incarnation in terms of the word or *logos*. These church traditions are of course not always reliable, and in the case of John's Gospel it is now obvious that much of its background is Jewish, and not Greek at all. If the prologue is removed from the gospel, there is little in the rest of it that actually demands a Greek background. Quite the reverse, in fact. The writer states his purpose in a very Jewish form: 'these things are written that you may believe that Jesus is the Christ (Messiah), the Son of God'. There is also an emphasis throughout the Gospel on the fulfilment of Old Testament sayings which again suggests a Jewish background.

This impression is confirmed by a closer analysis of the actual language of the gospel, for at many points the Greek language shows a close connection with Aramaic sources. The writer often uses Aramaic words – for example, *Cephas*, *Gabbatha*, or *Rabboni*, and then explains them for the benefit of his Greek readers. Even the meaning of the word Messiah is given a careful explanation.

More significantly, there are also a number of points at which the Greek of the gospel follows the rules of Aramaic grammar. An instance of this occurs when John the Baptist says of Jesus, 'I am not worthy that I should untie the thong of his sandals' (John 1:27). Though the distinction is not made in our English versions, the other gospels have a different, and correct, Greek expression, 'to untie'. But the unusual form of the statement in John is a regular idiom of the Aramaic language.

Then we also find Jesus' sayings in John expressed in the typical parallelism of Semitic poetry, and other sections of his teaching can be retranslated into Aramaic to form completely realistic Aramaic poetry.

It is not likely that John is a direct translation of an Aramaic document, though some have argued for this. But these facts do suggest that the teaching in John has the same Palestinian background as the material of the synoptic gospels; and the curious use of Aramaic grammar in Greek writing may well suggest that Aramaic was the author's native language.

## Archaeological Discoveries

In addition to the internal evidence, there is also a considerable and important body of evidence drawn from archaeology which makes the old idea that John was a late Hellenistic gospel now untenable. Three main pieces of evidence are important here.

The Dead Sea Scrolls have shown that the combination of Greek and Jewish ideas which we find in John was current not only in Greek cities like Ephesus in the 2nd century AD, but also in Palestine itself, in strict Jewish circles, in the pre-Christian era. Many phrases familiar from John are also found in the scrolls. 'Doing the truth' (John 3:21), 'walking in darkness' (John 12:35), 'sons of the light' (John 12:36), 'the Spirit of truth' (John 14:17), and many more expressions are as typical of the Qumran community as they are of John's Gospel. Moreover, the contrasts made in John between light and darkness, truth and error, are also typical of the Qumran texts.

And in both places this dualism between light and darkness, truth and error is an ethical dualism, in contrast to the metaphysical emphasis of most Greek and Gnostic philosophies.

Another discovery, of equal importance, and made at about the same time as the Dead Sea Scrolls, is the Coptic Gnostic library found at Nag Hammadi in upper Egypt. Prior to the discovery of these documents, Gnosticism was known mostly from the works of early church historians and theologians who wrote books to refute it. From their statements it was not too difficult to imagine that John's Gospel could have been written in the 2nd century as a part of the battle between Gnostic and 'orthodox' Christians. But direct access to the writings of Gnostic teachers has shown that there is a vast difference between the world of John's Gospel and the world of classical Gnosticism.

Archaeological excavations in Jerusalem have also provided evidence to illuminate the traditions of John's Gospel. One of the unusual features of this gospel is its proliferation of names and descriptions of places. It was widely thought at one time that these names were introduced either to serve as symbols for theological messages, or to give the impression of authenticity in otherwise fabricated accounts. But it is now clear that most of this geographical information rests on real knowledge of the city as it was before AD70. In that year the Romans so completely destroyed Jerusalem that it would have been impossible to observe the ruins later and imagine what the city must have been like beforehand. Excavations in Jerusalem have now shown that descriptions of the Pool of Bethesda, for example, or 'the Pavement' where Jesus met Pilate, are based on intimate knowledge of the city as it was in the time of Jesus.

## The Author and Date of Writing

The cumulative effect of all these converging lines of investigation has been to reinstate John's Gospel as a credible source for the life and teaching of Jesus. It has also re-opened the question of the authorship and date of this gospel. The matter of authorship has always been rather confused, not least because the church traditions mention two

Johns in connection with the gospel: the apostle, and a John who is called 'the Elder'. There is also the fact that the gospel itself seems to portray the 'beloved disciple' as a source of some of its information – though it never makes clear who this person was. Irenaeus identified the beloved disciple with John the apostle, but he could just as easily be an ideal figure, symbolic of any true follower of Christ. He has even been identified with Lazarus who is the only person of whom it is consistently said that Jesus loved him.

An attractive hypothesis that may explain the new facts now coming to light about John is the idea that this gospel has gone through two editions. We have already seen that apart from the prologue the gospel seems to be a very Jewish book, but with the prologue it takes on the appearance of a book more suited to the Greek world. It is therefore possible that the prologue was added after the completion of the original work, to commend the gospel to a new readership.

This possibility is also supported by the odd connection between chapters 20 and 21. The last verse of chapter 20 looks like the logical conclusion of the book, but it is then followed by the post-resurrection instructions of Jesus to Peter in chapter 21. This final chapter could also have been added at the time when the book was sent off to serve the needs of a new group of people, though its style and language is so close to that of the rest of the gospel that it must have been added by the same person.

It seems possible that the gospel was first written in Palestine, to demonstrate that 'Jesus is the Christ'. The author may have had in view sectarian Jews influenced by ideas like those of the Qumran community. Then, when the same teaching was seen to be relevant to people elsewhere in the Roman Empire, the gospel was revised: Jewish customs and expressions were explained, and the prologue and epilogue added. The advice to church leaders in chapter 21 suggests that the final form of the gospel may then have been directed to a Jewish Christian congregation somewhere in the Hellenistic world – perhaps, as church tradition says, in Ephesus.

The question of the date of the gospel is really wide open, because we have no other evidence against which to set it. The church Fathers imply that it was written by John the apostle at the end of a long life, and most scholars continue to date it somewhere between AD70 and 100. It must certainly not be dated later than the end of the 1st century, but there is no real evidence for dating it towards the end of that period. It has even been argued that it could be the earliest of all the gospels, written sometime between AD40 and 65. Some key themes of the gospel in its present form are related to the emergence of Docetism, which we know was not until later in the 1st century. So while much of the material of this gospel could well be from the same period as the synoptic gospels, it was probably edited into its present form a bit later – maybe around AD85. But there is no reason why the original authority for its content should not be John the apostle or one of his close associates.

## The Purpose and Structure of John

The gospel of John leaves us in no doubt as to the purpose of the book: 'Now Jesus did many other signs in the presence of his disciples, which are not written in this book. But these are written so that you may come to believe that Jesus is the Messiah, the Son of God, and that through believing you may have life in his name' (John 20:31). Three things clearly follow from this:

(a) the book was intended to be a purposeful presentation of Christian belief, aimed at convincing readers of its truth and inviting them to follow Jesus

(b) a major focus of the author's concern was to insist that true faith centres on the person of Jesus, understood as both 'Messiah' and 'Son of God'

(c) in order to achieve these objectives, the stories and teachings included in the gospel have been carefully selected from all that was known of the life and teaching of Jesus.

The fact that he had carefully selected appropriate materials must have been important to the author, as he later repeats the same claim (John 21:25). So if this is not intended to be a comprehensive account of all that Jesus said and did, what motivated him to make this particular selection? The answer to that question illuminates both the purpose and the structure of this gospel.

## Purpose

John's Gospel was part of a larger collection of works written by the same author, and including the three letters now known as 1, 2 and 3 John. The most significant of these letters is 1 John, and there is a good deal of debate as to whether that letter was written before or after the gospel. Either way, the two documents taken together clearly reveal their origin in a Christian community dominated by arguments about who Jesus was. Traditional Greek philosophy had always assumed that the world of spirit (where God could be found) was fundamentally incompatible with the world of material existence (where people live). So it was not long before Christians were wondering how Jesus could possibly have been both divine and human at the same time. Jesus' birth and death raised particular problems – for how could God either be born or die, and still be God? One way of answering that question was to suppose that Jesus had not really been human at all, but merely seemed to be so. This view came to be known as 'Docetism', from the Greek verb *dokeo*, meaning 'to seem'. One popular version of this view maintained that Jesus became divine at his baptism, but that the divine spirit left him before the crucifixion, making it possible to believe that God had really and truly been present in Jesus' life and teaching, without stumbling over philosophical questions about matter and spirit. The gospel does not address such matters as directly as 1 John, but its teaching has a clear relevance to them. So it insists that Jesus really did die on the cross (with real blood and water pouring from his body, John 19:34–35), and that the eternal word, or *logos* of Greek philosophical speculation truly 'became flesh' in the human person, Jesus of Nazareth (John 1:1–18).

## Structure

There is always an element of guesswork involved in trying to understand how an ancient author organized a particular work. But the gospel seems to have four main parts.

The Prologue (chapter 1): This sets the scene by introducing the main characters: John the Baptist and some of the leading disciples, but especially Jesus himself, who is described in elevated terms as the Word, Son of God, Christ (Messiah), the king of Israel, and the Son of Man. The chapter ends by affirming that the worlds of earth and heaven are not separate, but have been united by Jesus, thereby making it possible for those who follow him to share in the very life of God.

Miracles and Teaching (chapters 2–12): John always refers to Jesus' miracles as 'signs': for those with the faith to see it, what Jesus does and says reveals the character of God. Each of the miracles is accompanied by teaching which applies their meaning more widely to the experience of all who follow Jesus:

– the changing of water into wine (chapter 2) is related to the new life available to all (chapter 3)

– healing an official's son (chapter 4) is linked to teaching about the water of life (also chapter 4)

– healing a paralysed man at the pool of Bethesda (chapter 5) leads into teaching about Jesus as Son of God and life-giver

– feeding the 5,000 (chapter 6) is followed by teaching on the bread of life and the Spirit of Christ (chapters 6–7)

– teaching on Jesus as the light of life (chapter 8) prepares the way for the restoration of a blind man's sight (chapter 9)

– teaching on Jesus as the shepherd and life-giver (chapter 10) precedes the raising of Lazarus from the dead (chapter 11) and the claim that Jesus himself is 'the resurrection and the life' (11:25).

Jesus' Glorification (chapters 13–20): This is the story of Jesus' last meetings with his disciples, and of his death and resurrection – consistently referred to by John as Jesus' time of 'glory'. This theme is yet another way of reinforcing the belief that Jesus brought together the world of God and the world of humanity – and (contrary to Docetists and others) that this took place especially through his death and resurrection. This is why Jesus can be described as 'one with God' (10:30) as well as 'one with the church' (16:28).

The Epilogue (chapter 21): Here we find the seventh and final 'sign', the miraculous catching of fish by the disciples who had already fished all night, but caught nothing. This leads onto the recommissioning of Peter, and through him the other disciples, to take the message of Jesus out to the whole world – a mission that is rooted in the presentation of Jesus as Son of God and Messiah found in the previous chapters of the gospel.

*John Drane*

# THE GOSPEL OF ST JOHN IN LITERATURE

## Themes and Images

'Behold the Man'    20

Bethesda    23

Bread of Life    26

Lamb of God    28

Light    30

Thirst    34

Wedding at Cana    37

## Major Characters

Jesus Christ    42

John the Beloved Disciple    47

Judas Iscariot    49

Lazarus of Bethany    53

Mary Magdalene    57

Mary, Mother of Jesus    61

Nicodemus    68

Peter    71

Pontius Pilate    80

Thomas, Doubting    84

Woman of Samaria    86

Woman Taken in Adultery    88

## Themes and Images

### 'Behold the Man'

*'Idou ho anthropos'* (Latin *Ecce homo*, 'Behold the man') are the words used by Pilate in presenting Jesus to the Jews, bound, scourged, crowned with thorns, and wearing a purple robe (John 19:15). Most interpreters of Pilate's laconic statement have taken *Ecce homo* to mean, 'Here is the poor fellow!', the speaker's rhetoric having the purpose of eliciting pity from the spectators, or contemptuously ridiculing the Jews for taking such a lowly and risible figure's claim to kingship over them so seriously, or provoking them into demanding Christ's release. Among those exegetes interested in drawing out the theological implications of Pilate's pronouncement, some suggest that John here emphasizes the incarnation ('the man' reflects the messianic title 'Son of man'), while others equate the 'man of sorrows' (Isaiah 53:3) with Jesus in his humanity (*The Gospel According to John, xiii-xxi*, Anchor Bible, 1970, 876).

Only with the gradual proliferation of meditational and devotional writings in the Middle Ages, from Anselm of Canterbury's contemplations of Christ's sufferings and death in his Prayer to the Cross and *Cur Deus Homo?* in the 11th century to Thomas à Kempis' *Imitatio Christi* in the 15th, does the *Ecce homo* theme and its iconography become a marked feature in artistic expressions of Christian culture.

In the York 'Christ before Pilate: the Judgment', Pilate's *'Ecce homo'* introduces a 'fool-king' (434); the anonymous playwright effectively develops the drama built into the Johannine account of Christ's response to Pilate's 'Whence art thou?': 'But he gave him no answer' (19:9). Representations of the *Ecce homo* scene by Bosch and Dürer set precedents for treatments of the subject by Titian, Correggio, Tintoretto, Rubens, and Rembrandt, among many others. The frequency of these renderings has made a virtual genre of the subject, adding *Ecce homo* to the English lexicon, as a substantive for a picture of Christ wearing the crown of thorns.

The marked interest in the Passion which emerged during the

later Middle Ages continues among major writers of the English Renaissance, though their meditations tend to be more autobiographical. Donne's 'Spit in my face, yee Jewes', seventh of his *Holy Sonnets* of 1633, shows a characteristic double movement: the poetic divine identifies himself both with the reviled Christ and with those who continue to crucify him by their sinning. The closing couplet speaks of the Son of God's humility in taking on 'vile mans flesh', a theme Donne takes up again in *A Litanie*:

> Through thy submitting all, to blowes,
> Thy face, thy clothes to spoile; thy fame to scorne,
> All waies, which rage, or Justice knowes,
> And by which thou could'st shew, that thou wast born...
> (172–75)

In 'Out of Grotius his tragedy of Christes sufferinges', Crashaw calls up the image of Christ mocked at his trial, while in *Steps to the Temple* and *Carmen Deo Nostro*, he enters into sympathetic union with the suffering Christ even as he tearfully confesses his responsibility for the Passion. The Miltonic *Ecce homo* adds a political dimension to autobiographical reflection. Milton's Samson, a type of Christ as the Man of Sorrows and the Saviour, is pictured in the dual role of fool and champion: he is an object of pity to his people and of derision to the infidel. The Chorus in *Samson Agonistes*, at a loss to understand the inscrutable workings of providence, appeals to God to deliver the champion brought low: 'Behold him in this state calamitous' (708). God has pity in the end; the blind man in Gaza and theocracy prevail.

Like Milton's Samson, Blake's Christ is the great agent of revolution against Caesarism and all its works. In his annotations to Dr Thornton's 'New Translation of the Lord's Prayer', for example, Blake identifies Pilate with Caesar, the 'Learned', or the man of natural reason; and Christ with the 'Illiterate' man of the spirit or imagination who serves the 'Kingdom of Heaven'. Though Jesus does 'suffer himself to be Mock'd by Caesar's Soldiers Willingly', his proud silence pronounces the free spirit's anathema against the agents of science and rational ethics and the secular state these uphold. In the words of *Jerusalem*, the agonized Christ 'in weak & mortal clay' no

21

less shows the 'Form Divine', 'the Divine Vision' (stanza 18): Blake's Jesus is his fully realized visionary man. As Alfred Kazin remarks, Blake heralds something of the 'heroic vitalism' which impels the writings of Nietzsche and D.H. Lawrence (Introduction to *The Portable Blake*, 1946, 23). Nietzsche's autobiography, *Ecce Homo*, pictures the self-reliant divine man scornful of rational ethics and received values, while Lawrence's novella *The Man Who Died* imagines a Christ more vital if less heroic: 'the man' is grateful to 'Pilate and the high priests' for reminding him of his humanity.

Sir John Seeley's mid-Victorian *Ecce Homo: A Survey of the Life and Work of Jesus Christ* presents 'the man' as the greatest exemplar of moral virtue, whose teachings have been made insipid by the materialism of a church wed to the state. Seeley's *Ecce Homo* neither affirms nor denies Christ's divinity, but calls on the people of England to imitate Christ and thereby establish a republic of charity in which Christians will be governed solely by the moral imperatives dictated by the soul to each citizen. The problematic conjunction of church and state is also at issue, though indirectly, in Matthew Arnold's 'The Sick King in Bokhara', which seems to make use of the biblical *Ecce homo*: 'In the King's path, behold, the man' (94). Caught between the law and the spirit, duty and mercy, Arnold's king reluctantly condemns 'the man', a self-confessed lawbreaker, and gives him an opportunity to save himself, which the man refuses. The sick monarch himself buries the conscientious lawbreaker.

Browning's *The Ring and the Book* incorporates an extended and ingenious treatment of the *Ecce homo* theme. In book 8, Count Guido Franceschini's lawyer figures his guilty client before the papal civil court as the mocked Christ suffering in silence (657–59) and casts him in the role of 'Samson in Gaza… the antetype / Of Guido at Rome' (638–39). Guido's testimony in book 5 shows him assuming that posture for himself. Similarly and ironically, the prosecutor likens his method of presenting Guido's wife and innocent victim to that of a painter of sacred subjects. In 'Behold Pompilia' (9.162), Juris Doctor Johannes-Baptista Bottinius sees himself unveiling her Madonna-like portrait before the court. Pope Innocent implicitly confirms the verisimilitude of the prosecutor's rendering when he likens Guido to Barabbas and so casts the convicted murderer in the role of an

Antichrist (10.2175–78). The pope finally resists the temptation to unjust clemency: both Christian charity and civil law call for Guido's execution.

Other 19th-century references to Christ's trial are found in the appendix to Frederick Douglass' *Narrative of the Life of an American Slave*, where the autobiographer pictures his people as whipped and reviled drudges at the mercy of Pilate and Herod, who represent an unholy alliance of church and state; and in Hall Caine's novel *The Christian*, where the protagonist, unjustly accused of sedition and manslaughter, is likened to the mocked Christ (4.7) who maintains a calm and dignified silence before a court which serves Caesar more than God (4.12).

More recently, Conrad's *Nostromo* sardonically rewrites the biblical *Ecce homo*. 'He made no answer', records Hirsch's response to Sotillo's demand that the prisoner reveal the location of the hidden silver (3.9). And when the Jewish merchant suffering the strappado receives a blow from the frustrated Sotillo's riding whip, he spits in the face of his inquisitor, who shoots him without thinking and so loses the informant innocent in fact of any knowledge of the silver. Sotillo's pronouncement to the soldiers who respond to the gunfire, 'Behold a man who will never speak again', obliquely points to Nostromo, 'the man of the people' fully apprised of the silver's location and whose unintentional death by gunfire will keep the secret safe. In Faulkner's *A Fable*, a parable set in World War I, and pitting against each other the powers of life and death, love and hate, a corporal and his twelve companions are judged by a military court to be the ringleaders of a mutiny by an entire regiment. The generals are mistaken. The entire fable pictures not the man before Pilate, but humanity itself.

Camille R. La Bossiére
*University of Ottawa*

## Bethesda

The pool of Bethesda, near Jerusalem's Sheep Gate, is mentioned only in John 5:2, where it is described as the site of a miraculous healing (5:2–16). The pool was surrounded by five porticoes in which the sick waited for an angel to stir the water (John 5:3–4) and provide healing for the first to step into it. Here Jesus healed a man who, during his thirty-eight years of sickness, had never been helped into the pool. Since this healing took place on a Sabbath, the religious Jews sought to kill Jesus (5:16).

Early English literature appropriates the place name in various paraphrases of the Gospels, reflecting the variant spellings but generally preferring the form 'Bethsaida' (*Rushworth Gospel, West Saxon Gospels, Lindisfarne*). In the *Cursor Mundi* the Antichrist, it is predicted, will be fostered in Bethesda (22101).

The typological interpretation of the Bethesda event was soon secularized and led to frequent figurative uses which usually focused on one part of the narrative such as the troubling of the water, its healing powers, or the sick man's coming too late. Wordsworth compares Bethesda to the human heart, describing the poet's words as

> Words that can soothe, more than they agitate;
> Whose spirit, like the angel that went down
> Into Bethesda's pool, with healing virtue,
> Informs the fountain in the human breast
> Which by the visitation was disturbed. ('Lines Suggested by a
> Portrait from the Pencil of F. Stone', 124–28)

A.H. Clough's poem 'Bethesda: A Sequel' tells of a man who is sick of duty, of serving the world's desires. The poem ends in uncertainty about the nature of the pool's waters – 'Of Lethe were they, or Philosophy' – and about the possibility of the sick man's being healed prematurely by 'some more diviner stranger'.

Ironic use is made of the Bethesda story by Charlotte Brontë in *Jane Eyre*. According to Mr Brocklehurst, the hypocritical manager of Lowood Institution, young Jane has been sent there 'even as the Jews of old sent their diseased to the troubled pool of Bethesda'. He asks the teachers and superintendent 'not to allow the waters to stagnate round her' (chapter 7). In George Eliot's *Felix Holt* the town of Treby is to be turned into a fashionable watering-place and given the name of 'Bethesda Spa' – a name which is considered blasphemous by those who object to this plan (chapter 3).

The sick man's disappointment about always coming too late is echoed ironically by Samuel Butler, whose Theobald Pontifex feels 'like the impotent man at the pool of Bethesda'. He tries to meet young ladies but is 'almost immediately cut out by someone less bashful than himself' (The Way of All Flesh, chapter 10). Similar references to the sick man's belatedness can be found in Thomas Hardy's A Pair of Blue Eyes, chapter 30, and in his The Mayor of Casterbridge, chapter 10.

A more serious handling of the story by Herman Melville combines social protest with a (certain) Christian hope. Wellingborough Redburn compares the dockwall beggars of Liverpool to the Jewish cripples and offers up a prayer 'that some angel might descend, and turn the waters of the docks into an elixir, that would heal all their woes, and make them, man and woman, healthy and whole as their ancestors, Adam and Eve, in the garden' (Redburn, chapter 38).

In Villette Charlotte Brontë makes the pool representative of both the world and history: 'thousands lie round the pool, weeping and despairing, to see it, through slow years, stagnant. Long are the "times" of Heaven: the orbits of angel messengers seem wide to mortal vision' (chapter 17).

A late example of allegorizing is Cardinal Newman's sermon on the text. Identifying sickness with sin, he sees Bethesda as the 'waters of health', where a man who has been 'taken with the goods of this world' lies, 'unable to advance himself towards a cure, in consequence of his long habit'. Others pass him by, who are perhaps unable to help one who 'obstinately refuses to be comforted' (Parochial Sermons).

In 20th-century American literature Thornton Wilder, in The Angel That Troubled the Waters, dramatizes the urgent wish of the sick to be healed, and their feelings of envy and suspicion toward each other. When a physician arrives at Bethesda who wants only to be healed of his sin, he is denied the cure by the angel. The moral of the play is: 'In Love's service only the wounded soldiers can serve.' In 'Nocturne at Bethesda', a poem by African-American poet Arna Bontemps, the sick man's waiting for healing serves as an image of unfulfilled hope for racial equality:

This pool that once the angels troubled does not move.
No angel stirs it now, no Saviour comes
With healing in His hands to raise the sick
And bid the lame man leap upon the ground.

Manfred Siebald
*Johannes Gutenberg Universität, Mainz, Germany*

## Bread of Life

Bread is an extraordinarily rich symbol in the Bible, appearing as a figure for providential gifts – both physical and spiritual – as well as gifts of human hospitality. The word can be metonymic for solid food of any kind, but when referring to baking generally means wheat bread. In the Old Testament sanctuary it is only in connection with the jealousy offering that barley is even mentioned (Numbers 5:15). According to Numbers 6:15 it was the duty of a Nazarite after expiration of his vow to make a presentation at the sanctuary of a (wheat) bread offering. In the New Testament, however, it was barley loaves from a little boy's lunch which Jesus used to feed the multitudes (John 6:9); barley was less desirable, hence cheaper and more often used by peasants.

The *locus classicus* for New Testament iconography of bread is John 6, in which Jesus remonstrates with those who pursue him the day after the miracle of the loaves and fishes, hoping for another free meal, some alluding to the 'manna in the desert', the 'bread from heaven' which they attribute to Moses. Jesus says rather, 'My Father giveth you the true bread from heaven. For the bread of God is he which cometh down from heaven, and giveth life unto the world.' Still confused, they ask for 'this bread', imagining corporeal food, but Jesus startles them by saying, 'I am the bread of life; he that cometh to me shall never hunger; and he that believeth on me shall never thirst' (John 6:31–35). St Augustine's commentary *In Joannis Evangelium* sets the tone for Western tradition, which depends on an opposition of the corporeal bread of the Old Covenant and the spiritual bread of the New: 'They considered therefore the things promised by Moses, and they considered the things promised by

Christ. The former promised a full belly on earth, but of the meat which perished; the latter promised not the meat which perishes but that which endures unto eternal life' (25.12). To hunger after the bread which Christ offers – himself – is to express 'the hunger of the inner man', and 'consequently, he that hungers after this bread, hungers after righteousness – that righteousness which comes down, however, from heaven, the righteousness that God gives, not that which one works for on his own' (26.1). This notion appears to underlie the double irony of Herbert's narrator Jesus in 'The Sacrifice', who says of his adversaries, 'They do wish me dead, / Who cannot wish, except I give them bread' (6–7).

Augustine had been led to make an analogy of the incarnation – the Word made flesh (26.10) – and the bread of the Eucharist. Concerning the bread 'which comes down from heaven', he says: 'Manna signified this bread; God's altar signified this bread. Those were sacraments. In the sign they were diverse; in the thing which they signified they were alike' (26.12–20). The incarnational reference is echoed in numerous medieval lyrics which, inspired also by an Antonian iconography of the Virgin, makes her womb the oven in which the bread of life was baked (e.g., a eucharistic hymn by James Ryman [R. Greene, *The Early English Carols*, no. 318]: 'In virgyne Mary this brede was bake, / Whenne Criste of her manhoode did take'). Herbert develops the same idea in a different fashion: 'I could believe an Impanation / At the rate of an incarnation, / If thou hadst died for Bread' ('H. Communion', 25–28). Herbert's 'Prayer for after the Sermon' in *A Priest to the Temple* may reflect a tendency after the Reformation to identify eucharistic nourishment with the nourishment of expounded Scriptures: 'Lord, thou hast fed us with the bread of life' (290; cf. Matthew Poole, *Annotations upon the Holy Bible*, John 6:35ff.). A general conflation of all the spiritual senses as opposed to the simple literal 'staff of life' or 'daily bread' of the paternoster (Matthew 6:11) is common after the 19th century. Carlyle, in *Sartor Resartus*, says: 'A second man I honour, and still more highly: Him who is seen toiling for the spiritually indispensable; not daily bread, but the bread of life' (3.4).

David L. Jeffrey
*University of Ottawa*

## Lamb of God

Lamb of God is one of the messianic titles of Jesus, used of him by
John the Baptist (John 1:29–30). Throughout the book of
Revelation, Jesus is pictured as the Lamb (Revelation 5:6; 12:11;
13:8; 22:1). And in 1 Peter 1:19, the sacrifice of Jesus is likened to
that of a lamb 'without spot or blemish'. The key Old Testament
materials lying behind this New Testament application are the
slaughtered lamb of the Exodus, whose blood smeared on the
doorpost spared the Israelites from the judgment inflicted upon the
Egyptians (Exodus 12:3–13), the sacrificial lambs used in Old
Testament worship, and also the lamb symbolism in Isaiah 53:6–7,
where the 'suffering servant' of the Lord is likened to a lamb
prepared for slaughter, whose vicarious sacrifice atones for the sins of
wayward 'sheep'.

Identification of Jesus as both the lamb of God and suffering
servant receives frequent mention in the early church (see, e.g.,
1 Clement 16:7; Epistle of Barnabas 5:2). In early Christian
iconography the lamb pictured on the shoulders of Christ the good
shepherd symbolizes the lost and found soul, but can also signify
Christ himself as sacrificial victim. In the first quarter of the 8th
century the image of the lamb as a *figura* of Christ achieved even
greater prominence when Pope Sergius made the *Agnus Dei* a part of
the ordinary of the Mass: 'Lamb of God, who takes away the sin of the
world, have mercy upon us.'

Traditional scriptural interpretation of the lamb is reflected in
the writings of St Thomas More (*Confutation*, 5.617G; *Passion*,
1.1296, where the reference is to Revelation 5:1, 13) and in Spenser's
*Faerie Queene* (1.1.5; 1.10.42; 1.10.57). The sacrificial character of
the lamb of God is noted in Henry Constable's 'O Gracious
Shepherd', where the blood of Christ on Calvary is 'lamb-like, offered
to the butcher's block'. Richard Crashaw's 'In the Holy Nativity of
Our Lord God' ends with a chorus 'To thee, dread Lamb! whose love
must keep / The Shepherds, more than they, the sheep.'

The lamb is a crucial image in the poetry of Blake. His *Songs of
Innocence* is introduced by a poem centring on 'a song about a Lamb'
which makes its hearers 'weep with joy' ('Piping down the valleys

wild'). In Blake's famous 'Little Lamb, who made thee?' the answer given in his second stanza is:

> Little Lamb I'll tell thee,
> Little Lamb I'll tell thee!
> He is calléd by thy name,
> For he calls himself a Lamb:
> He is meek & he is mild,
> He became a little child:
> I a child & thou a lamb,
> We are calléd by his name.
> Little Lamb God bless thee.
> Little Lamb God bless thee.

Though apparently redolent with traditional biblical associations, the lamb is here a figure for childhood innocence rather than atoning sacrifice (the same shift is evident in the writings of Laurence Sterne).

The identification of the Lamb of God with the Passion still governs Melville's allusion in *Billy Budd*, where

> the vapoury fleece hanging in the east, was shot through with a soft glory as of the fleece of the Lamb of God seen in mystical vision, and simultaneously therewith, watched by the wedged mass of upturned faces, Billy ascended, and ascending took the full rose of the dawn.

Frequent, though often idiosyncratic, references to the biblical Lamb of God have continued to appear in the 20th century. Virginia Moseley (*Joyce and the Bible*, 1967, 91) has drawn attention to Bloom's identification of himself with the *Agnus Dei* in the Lestrygonians section of *Ulysses*. In 'Mary's Song', Sylvia Plath draws on Old Testament sacrificial imagery, setting the symbol of a roasting lamb against images of the Holocaust. Harley Ellison, in 'Ernest and the Machine God', unites the image of the sheep being led to the slaughter with humanity in service of the Machine God; the biblical God is here replaced by 'A New Testament of deities for the computerized age' and humanity becomes the lamb to be devoured or sacrificed upon the new altars. The Ghent altarpiece 'The

Adoration of the Lamb' provides a unifying symbol in Albert Camus' *La Chute* (*The Fall*).

Robert Farrell
*Cornell University*
Catherine Karkov
*Miami University of Ohio*

## Light

Light, the first creation of God ('Let there be light', Genesis 1:3), is also one of the most important and complex symbols in the Bible. Five principal uses of the symbol may be discerned from both Old Testament and New Testament texts.

First, light is frequently used to symbolize God himself (Psalms 4:6; 27:1; James 1:17; 1 John 1:5), and, by extension, his heavenly dwelling (Colossians 1:12; 1 Timothy 6:16; Revelation 22:5). God covers himself with light as with a garment (Psalm 104:2), and his 'dwelling' or Shekinah (cf. 1 Chronicles 3:21ff.) is said to be in splendoured light (cf. Sanhedrin 39a; Ber. 7a; Shabbat 22b; Numbers Rabba 7.8).

Second, light can suggest moral goodness or holiness, in contrast to moral darkness (Matthew 5:14; John 3:19–20; 12:36; Ephesians 5:8). To 'walk in the light' is to obey God's word (1 Samuel 2:5); his 'commandments enlighten the eyes' (Psalm 19:8). In talmudic teaching, whenever and wherever God's law is closely observed, a refulgence of the Shekinah spills over into the lives of his people.

Third, light pictures salvation (Psalm 27:1) and is linked especially with the redemptive activity of Christ, 'the light of the world' (Matthew 5:16; Luke 2:32; John 1:1–9; 8:12; 9:5). This light is not achieved through human wisdom or special knowledge (or, in Plato's analogy, by an ascent out of the cave of human ignorance) but descends into human darkness, unbidden, and radically transforms it.

Light also symbolizes truth and understanding, as opposed to error, ignorance, or folly (Psalm 119:105, 130; 2 Corinthians 4:6). In eschatological contexts, it is related to justice (Psalm 37:6; Micah 7:9; Zechariah 3:5).

Finally, light represents joy, God's favour, and life, in contrast to sorrow and death (Psalm 112:4; Proverbs 18–19; Isaiah 58:8). To 'see the light' can thus mean simply 'to live' (Job 3:10; 33:29; cf. Psalm 58:9).

Works of English literature which made indisputable use of the biblical images of light cluster in the Middle Ages and Renaissance and occur chiefly in poetry which depicts God and heaven. Among major medieval examples are Dante's *Divine Comedy*, the Middle English *Pearl*, and the anonymous *Cloud of Unknowing*. Light is a chief symbol of moral goodness in Spenser (the image appears over 300 times in *The Faerie Queene*), and it permeates the 17th-century devotional poetry of Henry Vaughan ('They are all gone into the world of light'), Richard Crashaw, and Thomas Traherne.

No poet made more extensive use of light in its full range of biblical meanings than Milton, especially in *Paradise Lost* (where the invocation to book 3 is an encomium addressed to light). Milton's use of light imagery, doubtless affected by his own blindness, was so influential in English poetry that he is the pivotal figure in the development traced by Josephine Miles: whereas before Milton such epithets as 'good', 'great', and 'true' were the dominant words denoting moral goodness, after Milton words such as 'bright' and 'light' became dominant.

A clear departure from the biblical perspective on light, however, is occasioned by emphasis on the 'light of reason' as supreme during the 18th-century Enlightenment. In Locke's psychology, Archbishop Tillotson's sermons, or Pope's *Essay on Man*, reason is no longer regarded as a divine gift enabling the rational creature to perceive and act upon God's laws written in Scripture and the obedient heart. Rather, as Whichcote's phrase has it, 'the spirit of man is the candle of the Lord': the light of the awakening human spirit creates the new world of human freedom as envisaged, for example, in Goethe's *Faust*. Light is no longer, as in Genesis 1, the condition of creation, but of human consciousness. Its full glory lies in the future, in a Utopia to be achieved by human effort – in England, Blake thought, by the unification of Albion. In such contexts light as a literary symbol often appears as physical sight in conflict or tension with inner vision. Hence the frequent appearance of blind

31

characters who, Tiresias-like, alone 'see the light'. (An ironic treatment of this theme occurs in Kipling's *The Light that Failed*.)

In numerous modern works a loss of belief in illumination through God's law (Psalm 119:105) or Christ (John 1:4–5; 2 Corinthians 4:6; Ephesians 5:14) occasions a felt need for alternative 'light' for human vision (e.g., Virginia Woolf, *To the Lighthouse*). With postmodern loss of confidence in the Enlightenment era's supreme standard of reason, both gnostic notions of higher light and neopagan attractions to darkness tend to displace or syncretize biblical notions of the 'light of the world' (cf. John 8:12; 9:5).

The biblical tradition extends, however, well beyond the Enlightenment, sometimes self-consciously opposing rationalist or gnostic usage. In the 18th century William Cowper's 'The Shining Light', 'The Light and Glory of the Word', 'Sometimes a light surprizes', and 'Light Shining out of Darkness' all bear witness to familiar biblical images; the latter hymn is an answer to those who think that human reason is sufficient light for the proper understanding of nature, concluding:

> Blind unbelief is sure to err
> And scan his work in vain;
> God is his own interpreter
> And he will make it plain.

For Cowper the rationalist's 'light' is itself clearly a gift of God, though unrecognized as such:

> Their fortitude and wisdom were a flame
> Celestial, though they knew not whence it came,
> Deriv'd from the same source of light and grace
> That guides the Christian in his swifter race. ('Truth', 531–34)

The Christian's advantage is 'the blaze of scripture light' (*Hope*, 298); he or she knows that in nature as well as Scripture, 'the just Creator condescends to write, / In beams of inextinguishable light' (*Hope*, 133–34).

The 19th century affords similar examples. John Henry

(Cardinal) Newman's 'The Pillar of the Cloud' (better known as 'Lead, Kindly Light') blends reference to Psalm 119:105 with the Exodus motif. A stronger use of Old Testament imagery from the same period is that of W. Chalmers Smith (1867):

> Immortal, invisible, God only wise,
> In light inaccessible, hid from our eyes,
> Most blessed, most glorious, the Ancient of Days
> Almighty, victorious, thy great Name we praise.
>
> Great Father of Glory, pure Father of Light,
> Thine angels adore thee, all veiling their sight;
> All laud we would render: O help us to see
> 'Tis only the splendour of light hideth thee.

For 20th-century poet Margaret Avison (*Sunblue*, 1978) the biblical image of light captures in metaphor the relationship not merely of God to the world but of human consciousness to its creator ('Light I' – 'the light has looked on Light'). God the Father's relationship to his Son is also expressed as more than mere reflection, but a closed circuit of reciprocal light:

> The circuit of the Son
> in glory falling
> not short
> and without clutching after
> His Being-in-Light…

Yet, to bring light into darkness Christ puts on 'the altar-animal form / and livery of Man / to serve men under orders'; then, returning with souls won from darkness, in freedom to God:

> this circuit celebrates the Father of Lights
> who glorifies this Son and all that He
> in glory sows
> of Light. ('The Circuit')

David Jones' reference in his *Anathemata* to those 'that have the Lord for your light' (1.75) is an evocation of Psalm 27:1, especially its Latin hymn setting (*Dominus illuminatio mea*) but more widely familiar in the King James Version English of Handel's anthem, 'The Lord is my light.'

David L. Jeffrey
*University of Ottawa*
Leland Ryken
*Wheaton College*

## Thirst

That the land of the Hebrews was a 'dry and thirsty land' (Psalm 63:1) accounts for much of the concrete background for related imagery in the Bible, especially where the typology of salvation and yearning for God is concerned. Just as God led his people through the wilderness, giving them water from the rock (Exodus 17:6; cf. Deuteronomy 8:15; Psalms 78:15–16; 105:40–41; Isaiah 43:20), protecting them from the perils of a barren land, so also he protects, refreshes, and saves the parched souls who thirst after spiritual salvation. In the analogy of the Psalmist, 'as the hart pants after the water brooks, so pants my soul after thee, O God. My soul thirsteth for God, for the living God: when shall I come and appear before God?' (Psalm 42:1–2). Hence in the New Testament 'Blessed are they who hunger and thirst after righteousness, for they shall be filled' (Matthew 5:6); as the Exodus people 'hungry and thirsty' were 'delivered out of their distresses' by the Lord (Psalm 107:5), so 'he that believeth on me shall never thirst' (John 6:35; cf. John 7:37; Revelation 7:16; 21:6–7). Invitations by God to 'drink freely' are invitations to the fullness of life and salvation which come in the context of a covenant relationship with God (Isaiah 55:1–3), so that the rock from which flows living water is explicitly identified in New Testament typology with Christ: 'And [our fathers] did all drink the same spiritual drink: for they drank of that spiritual Rock that followed them: and that Rock was Christ' (1 Corinthians 10:4).

New Testament imagery of thirst is incomprehensible outside of patterns established in Old Testament narrative and poetry, and the weight of these associations lends force to three subsequently influential New Testament pericopes. The most familiar is the incident recorded in John 4 of Jesus' conversation with the Samaritan woman by the well (a 'hospitality test' scene recalling the covenant narratives of Rebecca and Rachel [Genesis 24:13–21; 19:1–15]) in which a gracious and prejudice-subverting request for a drink of water occasions the opportunity to speak of satisfying a deeper thirst. Had the woman known who he was, Jesus tells the Samaritan, she would have asked of him, and he would have given her living water (John 4:10). For 'whosoever drinketh of this [well] water shall thirst again: but whosoever drinketh of the water that I shall give him shall never thirst' (John 4:13–14).

In John 7 Jesus is recorded as making the same claim in the Temple on the last day of the Feast of Tabernacles: 'If any man thirst, let him come unto me and drink. He that believeth on me, as the scripture hath said, out of his belly shall flow rivers of living water' (7:37–38). What Jesus says here (and later in chapter 8) is best understood in terms of the celebration of the Feast of Tabernacles, a feast associated with the triumphant 'day of the Lord' (Zechariah 9–14), in which living waters will flow out from Jerusalem to assuage all thirst (14:8). According to rabbinic traditions of the Tosepta, the texts read in conjunction with the Feast of Tabernacles were those relating to the rock in the desert (Exodus 17; Deuteronomy 8:15; Psalms 78:15–16; 105:40–41; 114:8; Isaiah 43:20; 44:3; 48:21). Among the ceremonies associated with the feast are prayers for rain, and on each of the seven mornings of the feast a procession went down to the fountain of Gihon on the southeast side of the temple hill. There a priest filled a golden pitcher with water, as the choir chanted in repetition Isaiah 12:3, 'With joy you will draw up water from the wells of salvation.' After the procession returned up to the Temple through the Water Gate, the water was poured through a silver funnel at the altar, running into the ground; on the seventh day, this occurred after the altar had been circumambulated seven times. It was at this solemn moment on the seventh day that Jesus stood up in the Temple court to proclaim himself the source of 'living water'.

A third crucial narrative moment comes in John 19:28 where, among the last words of Jesus from the cross, is recorded his parched cry, 'I thirst', reflecting the expiring thirst of the suffering servant voiced in the messianic Psalm 22. For St Augustine, that he was given vinegar was emblematic of the degeneration of his people from 'the wine of the patriarchs and prophets' (*In Joannis Evangelium Tractatus*, 119.4).

In medieval and Renaissance literature 'thirst' is often a figure for carnal desire. Lovers like those in Deduit's garden drink from the fountain whose waters are 'so sweet that there is no man who drinks of it who does not drink more than he should' even though 'those who go on drinking more burn with thirst than before... Lechery so stimulates them that they become hydroptic' (Guillaume de Lorris, Part I) and Jean de Meun (Part II), *Romance of the Rose*, translated by Dahlberg, 5979–98). 'For ay thurst I', says Troilus of love, 'the more that ich it drynke' (Chaucer, *Troilus and Criseyde*, 1.406). In the same vein, the persona of Donne's 'St Lucy's Day' imagines the whole earth to be 'hydroptic', so much does he long for his departed love.

Sometimes, however, the thirst may be the 'new thirst' Dante feels as he ascends the mount of Purgatory (*Purgatorio*, 18.3), the 'strong, sober thirst' Donne feels in 'La Corona' (1.12), or the thirst of Adam for Raphael's divine instructions, which 'bring to their sweetness no satiety' (Milton, *Paradise Lost*, 8.316).

In 18th- and 19th-century poetry the motif of spiritual thirst is commonplace: in the minor Victorian poet and Catholic convert Fredrick William Faber's 'The Shadow of the Rock', a weary pilgrim is invited 'Cool water to take / Thy thirst to slake' in clear reference to Exodus 17 and its attendant typologies. William Chatterton Dix's 'I Thirst' is a synthesis of relevant typologies:

> Weary beside the well he sat;
> Oh, who can tell but Jesus knew the thirst
> Which yet intenser grew, when on the cross
> For him no kindly fountain burst?
>
> 'I thirst', his spirit may have cried,
> Thus long before the Passion-hour drew nigh;
> Thirsting for souls who sought some cooling stream
> Yet passed the Living Water by. (stanzas 1–2)

In modern poetry 'dryness' or 'thirst' has become attached to intellectual or imaginative stagnation. Nevertheless, it is also in the sense of a spiritual drought that T.S. Eliot employs the motif in his *The Waste Land*, where the 'dry stone' with 'no sound of water' (1.24) is unmistakably revealed as the Rock in part 5, 'What the Thunder said'. Thirst prompts the persona's utterance ('If there were water we should stop and drink', 5.335), which is frustrated even as drawn onward by hope, the 'sound of water over a rock' (5.355). Eliot's thirst was to be quenched, he suggests, only when he could make the 'Journey of the Magi', eventually to discover 'the source of the longest river / The voice of the hidden waterfall' ('Little Gidding', 5.248–49).

David L. Jeffrey
*University of Ottawa*
H. David Brumble
*University of Pittsburgh*

## Wedding at Cana

Only the Gospel of John (2:1–11) reports the incident of Jesus' miraculous turning of water into wine at a wedding feast in the Galilean town of Cana. John locates the episode at the beginning of Christ's ministry, just after the baptism and temptation and the calling of the disciples, and just before the cleansing of the Temple (which John alone of the evangelists places at the beginning of the ministry). John notes at the end of the episode that this was the first of the miracles or signs wrought by Jesus (one of the seven mentioned in this Gospel) and that he thereby 'manifested forth his glory; and his disciples believed on him'. This helps to explain why the incident at Cana, along with the visit of the Magi and the baptism of Jesus, was originally associated with the ancient feast of Epiphany (January 6); in the Middle Ages Cana came to be celebrated by itself on the second Sunday after Epiphany.

Critical commentary has always focused on the implications of Jesus' attendance at the wedding, the import of the exchange between Jesus and his mother prior to the working of the miracle, and the purpose and significance of the miracle itself. While there are no explicit Old Testament allusions in the account, the miracle at Cana has been variously associated with several acts of Moses – procuring water from a rock (Exodus 17:1–7), making bitter water sweet (15:23–25), and turning water to blood (7:17–25) – and of Elisha and Elijah (1 Kings 17:1–16; 2 Kings 2:19–22; 4:1–7).

The Cana episode accords with much which is known about Near Eastern wedding customs, especially the importance ascribed to the provision of wine for the wedding feast; commonly the wine was diluted with water. The Christian liturgies, Eastern and Western both, have always placed special significance on the mingling of water and wine in the chalice for consecration, as a symbol of the unity of divine and human natures in the person of Jesus Christ (for examples from the Eastern liturgies see E.S. Drower, *Water into Wine*, 1956, chapters 4–5).

The first appearance of the Cana story in English poetry occurs in the Middle English verse paraphrases of Scripture, as in the *English Metrical Homilies* (199.1–121.16), the *Stanzaic Life of Christ* (1525–28, 1577–84), and, most elaborately, in the *Cursor Mundi* (13.360–13.451). The passage ends with reference to the apocryphal tradition that this was the wedding of John, who 'there laft the bridegome his bride & followed ihesu fra that tide'.

In *The Canterbury Tales*, Chaucer's Parson gives the usual exposition, that by his presence at the wedding Christ hallowed the institution of marriage, and he goes on to allegorize the miracle of the wine as Christ's transformation of the mortal sin of sexual intercourse into the merely venial sin it is in marriage (*The Parson's Tale*, 10.915–20). This reading is in marked contrast to the famous reference by the Wife of Bath, who indeed acknowledges that she was told:

> That sith that Crist ne wente evere but onis
> To weddyng, in the Cane of Galilee,
> That by the same ensample taughte he me
> That I ne sholde wedded be but ones.
> (*Wife of Bath's Tale*, Prologue 3.10–13)

She draws a connection with Jesus' message to the Samaritan woman at the well – but quickly demonstrates her inability to fathom these teachings ('What that he mente therby, I kan nat seyn').

In later English literature references to the Cana miracle occur frequently in religious contexts, but one also finds proverbial allusions to water changed to wine or 'saving the good wine until last'. A more direct allusion, by Herbert, occurs in 'Divinite', in which the association of the transformation of water into wine with the imparting of spiritual insight contrasts with theological speculation which only clouds such insight:

> Could not that Wisdome, which first broacht the wine,
> Have thicken'd it with definitions?
> And jagg'd his seamlesse coat, had that been fine,
> With curious questions and divisions? (9–12)

A baroque, quite secular allusion occurs in Herrick's 'To the Water Nymphs, drinking at the Fountain', in which the speaker bids the nymphs but touch the cup to their lips 'And I shall see by that one kisse, / The Water turn'd to Wine' (7–8). This playful image is reminiscent of a similar line in one of Crashaw's Latin Epigrams: 'Nympha pudica Deum vidit, & erubuit' ('The chaste nymph has seen [her] God and blushed'). Crashaw echoes the line in his translation 'Out of Grotius his Tragedy of Christes sufferinges':

> What would they more? th'ave seene when at my nod
> Great Natures selfe hath shrunke and spike mee god.
> Drinke fayling there where I a guest did shine
> The Water blush'd, and started into Wine. (49–52)

Curiously, the image is anticipated, almost exactly, by Caelius Sedulius (5th century): 'Now Cana sees in wonder new – / the water blushes at his view' (translated by H. Henry). A second Divine Epigram by Crashaw is based on the conceit that Christ's sinful enemy reverses the miracle by abusing wine and bringing on quarrels and tears:

> Thou water turn'st to Wine (faire friend of Life);
> Thy foe to crosse the sweet Arts of thy Reigne
> Distills from thence the Teares of wrath and strife,
> And so turnes wine to Water backe againe.

Several 19th-century poets make use of water-and-wine imagery in a romantic context in such a way as to leave uncertain whether any allusion to Cana is intended. In *Don Juan* Byron compares the sequence of love and marriage to the turning of wine to vinegar (3.5.5) and, with reference to drinking and drowning, speaks of a 'wine and watery grave' (2.57.5). Tennyson, following the now proverbial expression of saving the best wine till last, makes reference in 'The Grail' to Lancelot's being the last of Arthur's knights (757–60). A similar allusion occurs in Browning's 'Popularity' (stanza 4), with reference to the recognition of a poet. In G.M. Hopkins' 'Easter' the allusion retains its explicit religious context:

> Build His church and deck His shrine,
> Empty though it be on earth;
> Ye have kept your choicest wine –
> Let it flow for heavenly mirth.

In Browning's *The Ring and the Book*, Pompilia bitterly recalls how the cynical priest who conspired to marry her off to his brother Guido preached the doctrine of Cana to her:

> Read here and there, made me say that and this,
> And after, told me I was now a wife,
> Honoured indeed, since Christ thus weds the Church,
> And therefore turned he water into wine,
> To show I should obey my spouse like Christ. (7.445–49)

But her experience quickly teaches her that things are otherwise: 'Nothing is changed however, wine is wine / And water only water in our house' (7.474–75).

Treatments of and references to Cana continue to occur in modern religious poetry, for example, in Edgar Lee Masters' 'The Wedding Feast', which builds strongly on the exegetical tradition, with references to Moses' striking water from a rock (stanza 7), Elisha's provision of oil for a widow (stanza 8), and the supplanting of Old Testament signs with new spiritual doctrine (*Selected Poems*, 1925, 238–40). Sister Mary Edwin's collection of verse *Water into*

*Wine* (1928) utilizes the Cana theme not only in the Proem and title poem but also in the poem 'Marriage in Galilee'.

The Cana miracle is also dealt with in Dorothy L. Sayers' radio play 'A Certain Nobleman', one of the series *The Man Born to Be King* (1943). Another pious modern paraphrase is Agnes Turnbull's short story 'The Miracle of Cana' (from the collection *Far Above Rubies*, reprinted in Cynthia Maus, *Christ and the Fine Arts*, 1938, 269–76). In Emil Ludwig's *Son of Man* (1928), the miracle is treated as an illusion effected by Jesus' hypnotic powers.

Douglas' *The Robe* (1942) illustrates the struggle of modern piety with the idea of miracles, introducing every conceivable rationalistic explanation for Jesus' miracles through the reflections of Marcellus, the Roman centurion. Regarding the miracle at Cana, Marcellus at first explores the explanation that the water had been poured into jars which had been used for storing wine, but eventually rationalization shifts into allegorization reminiscent of Chrysostom, as Marcellus comes to see that transformation of attitude and personality is even more of a miracle than the changing of water into wine.

Robert Graves' novel *King Jesus* (1946) presents the incident at Cana as a moral demonstration by Jesus which has subsequently come to be distorted and interpreted precisely contrary to Jesus' intent. What Jesus did, as Graves tells it, was to command that the jars of purification be filled with water, which he then drank, declaring that to be the true wine Adam drank in Eden: 'The master of ceremonies followed his example and swore that never had he tasted such good wine. He meant that he approved Jesus' message: Cleanliness, that is to say "holiness before the Lord", is better than excessive drinking.' In substituting lustral water for wine, Jesus was also saying 'that Adam and Eve in the days of innocency abstained from carnal love – of which the emblem in the Song of Solomon is wine' (293). More orthodox treatments of the Cana miracle abound in the host of modern novelizations of the life of Christ.

George L. Scheper
*Essex Community College and
John Hopkins University School of Continuing Study*

## Major Characters

### Jesus Christ

The name Jesus comes from the Greek *Iesous*, the adaptation of the Hebrew name *Yehoshua* (Aramaic *Yeshua*), the name of the great hero of the conquest of Canaan, familiar to Old Testament readers as Joshua. The term 'Christ' is adapted from the Greek *Christos*, which translates the Hebrew *mashiah* (from which the term 'Messiah' is derived), meaning 'anointed'. Christ is thus originally not a name but a title reflecting the early Christian conviction that Jesus is the Messiah, the 'anointed one', who fulfils the hope for a God-sent saviour.

The four Gospels of the New Testament are our major source of information about Jesus of Nazareth and the primary basis for the picture of him which is accepted by traditional Christianity. Commonly dated by scholars between AD65 and 95, they are also recognized as embodying the Jesus tradition of much earlier years. With the rise of modern historicism, especially in the 19th century, many strove to construct a somewhat detailed, chronologically arranged life of Jesus from the Gospels. A. Schweitzer's classic *The Quest of the Historical Jesus* traces the failure of this enterprise, and New Testament scholars today recognize that the gospels (like all ancient biographical literature) were not written to provide a chronological or developmental account of their subject but were intended as collections of Jesus tradition and interpretations of him for the religious needs of 1st-century churches. Nevertheless, nearly all New Testament scholars today are persuaded that, although a detailed life of Jesus cannot be written, the Gospels do provide a basis for a more modest historical description of Jesus' ministry and message which accords with the standards of modern historical criticism.

John Milton (1608–74) is perhaps the most important English contributor to the literature about Jesus Christ. In *Paradise Lost* (published 1667) Milton assigns a significant part of the process of creation to God the Son. God the Father in effect withdraws, and the Word, God the Son, shapes the universe from the unformed matter which had originated with the Father. Underlying this Christian interpretation of the Genesis creation account is the Johannine conception of Jesus as the *Logos*, who existed from all eternity. Jesus as saviour and redeemer is the hero of *Paradise Regained* (published 1671). Milton concentrates on the Gospel accounts of Jesus' Baptism, the proclamation that he is the Son of God, and his heroic overcoming of the temptations of Satan.

The first significant 18th-century contributor to the literature of Jesus was Sir Richard Steele, who proposed in his literary manual of ethics entitled *The Christian Hero* (1701) that the best preceptor of conscience was Christ rather than any of the classical philosophers. Alexander Pope's *Messiah* (1712), a sacred eclogue on the messianic prophecies of Isaiah, is a noteworthy presentation of Old Testament prophetic expectations, understood as having their fulfilment in Christ.

It was not until the 19th century that Jesus and Jesus-like heroes became incorporated in the novel. This development was partly an offshoot of Christian socialism. Its first two exemplars were Elizabeth Linton's *The True History of Joshua Davidson* (1872) and Elizabeth S. Phelps Ward's *A Singular Life* (1895). Both present a socialistic hero. Linton's Joshua Davidson, the son of a carpenter in a small Cornish village, comes to London and there meets Félix Pyat, clearly meant to represent Karl Marx. A prostitute whom Joshua helps, Mary Prinsep, is the counterpart of Mary Magdalene. Joshua is eventually trampled to death by a London crowd when he vainly attempts to convince them that Christ and his apostles were communists. The implication of this rather awkwardly written novel is that, if Jesus were alive today, he would be an egalitarian working man with a provincial accent and a home in the slums of London who would vituperate against capitalists, landlords, Sabbatarians, bishops, and residents of the West End. Less extreme in her views, the American author Elizabeth Phelps proposes as her Jesus hero in *A Singular Life* a young clergyman, Emanuel Bayard, whose late father, Joseph, a clergyman and carpenter, had married his wife, Mary, in the New England village of Bethlehem. Emanuel's theology is not impeccably orthodox, so his application for the pastorate of the wealthy church of Windover is turned down by the congregation. Instead, he remains to minister to the poor fisherfolk of the town. He practises Christian socialism for the rest of his brief life, advocates teetotalism, and causes a scandal by befriending a local prostitute named Lena. By the age of 33, having alienated the town fathers and the local liquor interests beyond reconciliation, he dies as the result of being struck by a stone hurled at him by a grog-shop owner nicknamed Judas. Both of these novels are characterized by rigorous attention to the chronological sequence in the gospels, by their undisguised moral earnestness, and by their obvious highlighting of the biblical parallels.

Writers of this genre in the 20th century have been generally more sophisticated. John Steinbeck's *The Grapes of Wrath* (1939) recounts the exodus-like wanderings of the poverty-stricken Joad family, who leave the Oklahoma dust bowl with a horde of others like them and set out for California in an old, dilapidated car. Set against this Old Testament pattern is a secondary motif derived from the New Testament, involving a leader with the same initials as Jesus Christ – Jim Casy – and his twelve fellow migrants, the Joad family. Casy is a former preacher who gradually moves from being an orthodox revivalist Christian to being a believer in the essential sanctity of man. While his religious thinking is slowly changing, Casy goes to prison to protect Tom Joad. Shortly after his release, he is killed by one of a group of antiunion men who hate his intentions. His attitude toward his attackers is epitomized in the words 'You don't know what you're a-doin', words which echo Jesus' appeal on the cross, 'Forgive them, Father, they know not what they do.'

Graham Greene's *The Power and the Glory* (1940) has as its hero a nameless whisky priest. Shifty and alcoholic, he lives in the virtually Marxist state of Tabasco in Mexico. His antagonist, the police lieutenant, is a fanatical atheist; he has all the fervour about his beliefs which the priest should have but lacks. The priest is ultimately executed by the state; he gives up his life for the sake of the criminal James Calver, a bank robber and murderer whose name suggests Calvary. Peter's denial of Jesus is symbolized by Padre José, who refuses to hear the whisky priest's confession, and Judas is represented by the mestizo, who in effect causes the hero's arrest.

The Jesus hero of Harold Kampf's *When He Shall Appear* (1953) is Janek Lazar, a Russian Jew living in London, who practises faith healing, gains disciples, and preaches a religion of simplicity. He is convinced that Christianity has become too dogmatic and has ceased to be a way of life. The clergy of all denominations unite against him, and he is subsequently arrested on a Thursday in the gardens of Leicester Square. Though the judge dismisses the charges, the clergy plot to have him banished. They are eventually successful, and Lazar is deported to Russia.

The Christ motif appears in a number of William Faulkner's works but nowhere more directly than in *A Fable* (1954). The Jesus figure here is the corporal, whose name, Stephan, is mentioned only once, after his death. Born at Christmas in a Middle Eastern stable, he associates himself with twelve men of his squadron and is executed at the age of 33. Parallels with the Gospel accounts are ubiquitous: they include a Judas figure, Polchek, who commits suicide by hanging himself, and two women who claim the corporal's body after his death, Marthe and Marya.

Gore Vidal's novel *Messiah* (1954; somewhat revised in later editions) is to a considerable degree a parodic reflection on the spread of 1st-century Christianity. The central character, John Cave, is a mortician from the state of Washington who comes south to California at the age of 30 and preaches that life on this earth is not worth living and that it is good to die. Suicide thus becomes a supremely virtuous act, provided that this 'better way' is chosen for the proper reasons. Cave quickly develops a huge following, and millions express their belief in Cavesword or Cavesway, the new religion, created largely by publicity agents, which soon displaces Christianity. Cave himself writes nothing, but his brilliant follower, Paul Himmell, publicizes Cave's oral teachings. Three years after Cave's arrival in California Himmell arranges to have him murdered and cremated and his ashes spread over the United States from a jet plane. Subsequently a special Congressional hearing proclaims Cavesword as the national religion.

John Barth's *Giles Goat-Boy or, The Revised New Syllabus* (1966) is also a parodic novel. The long and complicated plot evolves in a hypothetical university world controlled by the heartless computer WESCAC. The Shepherd Emeritus, Enos Enoch, is analogous to Jesus, and George Giles, by imitating him, constitutes a secondary

Jesus figure, whose mission in life is to redeem the university. The Virgin Mary, John the Baptist, Pontius Pilate, Mary Magdalene, and other biblical figures are represented by roughly comparable characters. This protracted and irreverent work constitutes in effect an undisguised literary caricature of Jesus and his followers.

An entirely different category of Jesus literature is devoted to stories of imaginary appearances of Jesus in modern times: early examples include an interpolated episode in Archibald McCowan's novel *Christ, the Socialist* (1894), William Stead's *If Christ Came to Chicago* (1894), and Edward Everett Hale's response to Stead, *If Christ Came to Boston* (1895). Jerome K. Jerome's play *The Passing of the Third Floor Back* (1907) presents a Jesus who lives in a London boarding house and works miracles for the benefit of his fellow lodgers. Perhaps the most meritorious contribution of this kind is Upton Sinclair's novel *They Call Me Carpenter* (1922), in which the narrator, having fallen unconscious in a church in Western City, dreams that Jesus steps down from a stained-glass window and enters public life under the name of Mr Carpenter. He supports a strike by the local tailor's union and is befriended by a film star named Mary Magna. Later he is betrayed by an agent of the American Legion posing as one of his disciples and is ordered to appear in the court of Judge Ponty. Before the trial takes place, the narrator's dream comes to an end.

A few inspirational novels in English present heroes who deliberately attempt to pattern their lives on what they believe Jesus would have done had he been in their place. The two best-known examples of this genre are Mary Augusta Ward's *Robert Elsmere* (1888), the tale of an English vicar who leaves his parish to form a 'New Brotherhood' of working men in the slums of London, and Charles Sheldon's *In His Steps, or What Would Jesus Do?* (1896), which tells of an American Congregationalist minister's campaign to persuade his followers not to do anything without first asking themselves 'What would Jesus do?' Glenn Clark's sequel to this novel, entitled *What Would Jesus Do?* (1950), incorporates a similar moral ideal for readers living in the post-World War II era.

Jesus has also been the subject of a number of 20th-century radio plays, films, and television series. These generally make no pretence to literary worth, but among the exceptions are Dorothy L. Sayers' *The Man Born to Be King* (1943) for radio and Anthony Burgess' *Jesus of Nazareth* (1977) for television.

David Greenwood
*University of Maryland*
Larry W. Hurtado
*University of Manitoba*

## John the Beloved Disciple

John the 'beloved disciple' (John 13:23), also called by later writers 'St John the Divine', was one of the sons of Zebedee and probably the younger brother of James. James and John, early followers of Jesus, were by him named 'Boanerges' ('sons of thunder'). Along with St Peter they accompanied Jesus on three important occasions: the raising of Jairus' daughter (Mark 5:37), the transfiguration (Matthew 17:1), and the night of prayer in the garden of Gethsemane (Mark 14:32–33). John was, after the resurrection and ascension, one of the leaders of the Christian community in Jerusalem. St Irenaeus reports that he lived to be an old age, composing his gospel in Ephesus. It has been conjectured that he incurred banishment under Emperor Domitian or Trajan, to Patmos, where he composed the Apocalypse attributed to him sometime between AD95 and 98. St Jerome records a tradition identifying John as the bridegroom of the marriage at Cana; in medieval *legenda* the bride is sometimes said to be Mary Magdalene. John's iconographic attributes include a scroll with the words *In principio erat Verbum* (from the Vulgate rendering of the first verse of his Gospel) and an eagle. He is normally depicted with a long beard, although in representations emphasizing his friendship with Jesus he can appear also as a handsome youth. Because of his association with *amicitia spiritualis*, perhaps, he becomes the addressee of the elegant *'Verbum Dei, Deo Natum'*, a poem by an anonymous writer of the circle of Adam of St Victor, in which he is associated with 'Ezekiel's eagle', sent to the Bride of Christ to bear 'of him whom thou didst loue so well, / Glad tidings' (translated by E.H. Plumptre). These associations may lie behind some of the imagery in Chaucer's *The House of Fame*.

47

On the cross Jesus, near death, commended John to his mother: 'Woman, behold thy son!' and then addressed his disciple, saying, 'Behold thy mother!' 'And from that hour that disciple took her unto his own home' (John 19:26–27). In his *De Amicitia Spirituali*, Aelred of Rievaulx contrasts the personalities of John and Peter, suggesting that the characteristic strengths of each were revealed in the fact that 'to Peter he gave the keys of his kingdom; to John he revealed the secrets of his heart. Peter, therefore, was the more exalted; John, the more secure... Peter... was exposed to action, John was reserved for love' (3.117). The force of the contrast, like that commonly made between Martha and Mary or Leah and Rachel, is to associate 'the beloved disciple' with the contemplative life. The intimate friendship of Jesus and John is also compared to that of David and Jonathan, as is still evident in Herbert's 'The Church-Porch' (271–76), where advice for Christ-like conduct is given:

> Thy friend put in thy bosome: wear his eies
> Still in thy heart, that he may see what's there.
> If cause require, thou art his sacrifice;
> Thy drops of bloud must pay down all his fear:
> But love is lost, the way of friendship's gone,
> Though *David* had his *Jonathan, Christ* his *John*.

These and other elements of John's character and role are developed in medieval *legenda*, notably in the Franciscan *Meditations on the Life of Christ*, of which Nicholas Love's *Mirrour of the Blessed Lyf of Jesu Christ* (circa 1400) was a popular Middle English translation. The Calvary scene lies behind Jacopone da Todi's widely adapted poem *Stabat Mater*, the commendation of Mary to John being popularized in Middle English lyrics such as 'Maiden & moder, cum & se' and N-Town, where it is amplified considerably as a three-way conversation between Jesus, Mary, and John (891–962).

In Dante's *Commedia* Peter, James, and John are representatives of faith, hope, and charity respectively, and examine the pilgrim Dante to assure that he understands the importance of these qualities (*Paradiso*, 24–26).

David L. Jeffrey
*University of Ottawa*

# Judas Iscariot

Judas Iscariot (perhaps 'Judah from the city of Keriyot' [in Judea; see Joshua 15:25]) is first mentioned in the Synoptic Gospels; in each instance he is identified as the betrayer of Jesus, his name coming at the end of a list of the apostles (Matthew 10:4; Mark 3:19; Luke 6:16). In the Gospel of John Judas is identified by Jesus himself as 'a devil' among the apostles (6:70–71). John also records that Judas was in charge of the common purse, from which he pilfered money (12:1–6; 13:29). All four Gospels tell how Judas led a band of Roman soldiers to arrest Jesus. In the Synoptic accounts (Matthew 26:49; Mark 14:45; Luke 22:47) he identifies Jesus for the authorities by kissing him; in John's Gospel Jesus declares himself (18:5). Only Matthew mentions the thirty pieces of silver paid to Judas by the chief priests for betraying his master (26:15), and he alone recounts Judas' 'repentance' and suicide by hanging (27:1–8). According to Acts 1:16–20 Judas died, apparently unrepentant, having bought a plot of land called 'Aceldama, that is to say, the field of blood' with his thirty pieces of silver, where 'falling headlong, he burst asunder in the midst, and all his bowels gushed out'.

There are references by St Irenaeus, Tertullian, and St Epiphanius to a no-longer-extant apocryphal Gospel of Judas in which Judas was portrayed as the enlightened secret agent of the redeemer who by his 'treachery' foiled the evil designs of demonic powers ('the Archons') to prevent the salvation of mankind. According to the Fathers and later medieval exegetes, however, Judas was driven by avarice and betrayed Christ of his own free will. In spite of his heinous crime he might still have been saved were it not for his desperate act of suicide. St Jerome, for example, argues that 'Judas offended the Lord more by hanging himself than by betraying Him' (Psalm 108; cf. also St Ambrose, De poenitentia, 2.4.27; St Augustine, De civitate Dei, 1.17; St Gregory the Great, Moralia in Iob, 11.12; and the Venerable Bede, In Lucam, 6.16). The association of the name and character of the avaricious and traitorous 'Judas' with the name and qualities of the 'Jew' is a medieval commonplace which has explicit patristic authority. According to Jerome, 'The Jews take their name, not from that Judah who was a holy man, but from the betrayer. From the former, we [i.e., Christians] are spiritual Jews; from the traitor come the carnal Jews' (*Homily* on Psalm 108).

Protestant exegesis of the Judas narrative is for the most part continuous with medieval tradition. Judas becomes a focus, however, of the theological debate concerning free will. Erasmus believed that Judas was free to change his intention (*De Libero Arbitrio*, 2), but Luther argued in rebuttal that Judas' will was immutable (*De Servo Arbitrio*, 1931, 1943, 1:323, 238; 5:200). Calvin states unequivocally that Judas was predestined to damnation (*Institutes*, 3.24.9), but writes on the question of Judas' guilt: 'surely in Judas' betrayal it will be no more right, because God himself both willed that his son be delivered up and delivered him up to death, to ascribe the guilt of the crime to God than to transfer the credit for redemption to Judas'. Concerning Judas' repentance he says, 'because [he] conceived of God only as Avenger and Judge... [his] repentance was nothing but a sort of entryway of hell' (*Institutes*, 1.18.4 and 3.3.4).

In the Old English *Elene*, Cynewulf's poetic retelling of the *inventio crucis* legend, the leader of the Jews and arch-antagonist of Helena, mother of Constantine, is named Judas. At first he misleads Helena but then 'betrays' his people by revealing the whereabouts of the True Cross and is converted. In a 13th-century variant of this story in the Middle English metrical biblical narrative *Cursor Mundi* Judas appears as a prototype of Shylock, demanding a pound of flesh from a goldsmith in Helena's circle who owes him money.

The Anglo-Norman *Voyage of St Brendan* (circa 1121) includes an elaborate account of the meeting between the saint and Judas. The biblical traitor describes in detail his torments in hell and explains that he is granted respite on certain Sundays of the year as a reward for small acts of charity he had performed. Judas' piteous laments, Brendan's grief, and the terrible torments which Judas describes are additions to the earlier Celtic and Latin versions of the Judas episode in the Brendan legend; the poet (Benedict of Gloucester?) has added these and other details to evoke sympathy for Judas, or at least to convey a terrifying object lesson by heightening the pathos of Judas' plight. This glimpse of the afterlife of Judas is repeated in the Middle English Brendan legend. The legendary life of Judas – from his birth and *enfance* to his eventual suicide, including the pseudo-Oedipal story of how he came to be an honoured member of Pilate's court, unwittingly murdered his father and married his mother, sought out Jesus to seek pardon for his sins, and became an apostle – is recounted in the popular late-13th-century *Legenda Aurea* by Jacobus de Voragine (translated in the 15th century by Caxton).

The 13th-century ballad of *Judas* depicts the biblical traitor as a tortured, pathetic figure who is manipulated by his sister and the Jew (*sic*) Pilate. On Holy Thursday Jesus gives Judas thirty pieces of silver and sends him off to buy food for the Passover feast. The red-bearded Judas meets his sister, who berates him for following Jesus, enchants him into falling asleep in her lap, and steals the money which Jesus entrusted to him. To recover the sum Judas perversely agrees to betray his master to Pilate.

In the ninth circle of Dante's *Inferno* Judas has pride of place in a triumvirate of traitors which also includes Brutus and Cassius. Judas' feet dangle while his head and upper torso are chewed eternally by the front mouth of Lucifer's three faces. The subdivision of the ninth circle of hell where this takes place is called *la Giudecca*, after Judas, a name which was also subsequently used for the Jewish ghettos of Europe. The linking of Judas and the Jews at large (as by Jerome, cited above) is also frequent in medieval art, by way of stereotypical details: red hair and beard, ruddy skin, yellow robe and money bag, large, hooked nose, big lips, and bleary eyes. In the early Middle English Peterborough Chronicle Judas and the Jews are linked in the annal for the year 1137, which states that 'Iudeus of Noruuic' crucified a Christian child (St William of Norwich). Langland in *Piers Plowman* (C.2.64) also stresses the Judas–Jews connection, alluding at the same time to the popular tradition that Judas hanged himself upon an elder tree. Similar references occur in Mandeville's *Travels*, Shakespeare's *Love's Labour's Lost*, 5.2.610, and Jonson's *Every Man Out of His Humour*, 4.4: 'He shall be your *Judas*, and you shall be his *elder-tree* to hang on.'

In *The Friar's Tale* (3.350) Chaucer refers to Judas as a 'theef' with 'little money bags' who kept back half of his master's due; and elsewhere in the *Canterbury Tales* Chaucer names Judas as the proverbial hypocrite and traitor (e.g., 7.3227; 8.1001–03), while in *The Parson's Tale* (10.502) Judas is adduced as an example of *grucching* brought on by avarice – a reference to John 12:4–6. Other references to Judas as the archetypal traitor and hypocrite, by writers from the Middle Ages to the present day, are far too numerous to list. This constitutes the predominant – and least interesting – significance assigned to the figure of Judas in the English tradition (e.g., in Emily Brontë's *Wuthering Heights*, the Bible-thumping Nelly Dean shouts down from the kitchen window at Heathcliff, who has just embraced Isabella Linton: 'Judas! traitor!... You are a hypocrite, too, are you? A deliberate deceiver'; and in Robert Penn Warren's *All the King's Men* (1946) the hero, Willie Stark, turns on two corrupt associates, the politician Duffy and the contractor Gummy Larson, accusing them of being like 'Judas Iscariot').

In medieval English drama Judas is regularly portrayed as an exemplary case of avarice and treason followed by despair. Three of the four English cycles – Wakefield, Chester, and York – show how Judas was driven by greed to betray Jesus. The suicide of Judas figures in the York and N-Town cycles, both of which follow the account in Matthew fairly closely. According to the popular homiletic view reflected in the latter two plays, as well as in the Wakefield play on the harrowing of hell and the *Southern Passion*, it was Judas' suicide rather than his betrayal which led to his eternal damnation. The Wakefield cycle also includes an incomplete play on Judas' suicide, *The Hanging of Judas*, of which all that survives is a monologue of about 100 lines in which Judas recounts a fantastic case-history, consisting of the same stock romance motifs from the Oedipus and Moses stories that appear in the *Legenda Aurea*. In addition to its slight but lurid narrative interest the fragment includes a lament of Judas which vividly conveys the pathos of his fate.

The medieval Judas legend continued to circulate in England well into the 18th century, when it was widely distributed in five distinct versions in several editions of chapbooks and in ballads. Jonathan Swift's poem 'Judas' is a satire on Irish clergy of the Church of England. The major development in the history of Judas in the 19th century is the emergence of a sympathetic treatment of him, based not on the sentimentalities of the apocryphal tradition but on a critical, rationalist reading of his New Testament role, most notably in David Friedrich Strauss' *Das Leben Jesu* (1835), translated by George Eliot

(1846). This may be the spirit which informs Matthew Arnold's portrayal of Judas in 'St Brendan' (1860), a poem which reverts to the medieval legend but eschews its sentimentality. St Brendan, sailing near the north pole on Christmas Eve, comes upon a red-haired Judas with 'furtive mien' and 'scowling eye' atop an iceberg, who relates how every Christmas he is granted an hour's respite from the flames of hell because he once gave his cloak to a leper. Arnold reduces the amount of relief granted Judas and highlights the traditional saints' life motif of the cloak and the leper. Richard Henry Horne's *Judas Iscariot* is a 19th-century miracle play. Robert Buchanan's *Judas Iscariot* is a powerful dramatization which adheres more closely than many to the New Testament narrative; Thomas Sturge Moore's dramatic effort of fifty years later, *Judas* (1923), is as powerful, but more textually dense and obscure.

George Russell (AE), in his poem 'Germinal', suggests a Freudian perspective on Judas' childhood: 'In the lost boyhood of Judas / Christ was betrayed.' In a variety of modern revisionist versions of the Gospel narrative – for example, Anthony Burgess' *Jesus of Nazareth*; George Moore's *The Brook Kerith*; Robert Graves' *King Jesus*; and Nicos Kazantzakis' *The Greek Passion* and *The Last Temptation of Christ* – Judas is absolved of the guilt associated with Christ's betrayal and passion, and accorded semi-heroic status. In Norman Mailer's *The Executioner's Song* (1980), the old gnostic view of Judas finds a fitting exponent in Gary Gilmore, the confessed murderer. When one of his lawyers says 'I feel like Judas helping you get executed,' the text continues:

> 'Judas,' said Gary, 'was the most bum-beefed man in history.' Judas knew what was going down, Gilmore said. Judas was there to help Jesus tune into prophecy.

> Lawrence Besserman
> *Hebrew University of Jerusalem*

## Lazarus of Bethany

Lazarus, brother of Martha and Mary and friend of Jesus, lived at Bethany in Judea and was resurrected by Jesus after having been dead for four days (John 11:1–44). When the sisters notified Jesus of Lazarus' sickness, Jesus waited two days, so that God might be glorified by the miracle to happen (11:40) and so that people's belief in his divine mission might be strengthened (11:15, 42). At the tomb, Jesus wept, and then, after praying, called Lazarus forth from death. This miracle, seen by many scholars as the seventh and concluding 'sign' in the Johannine 'book of signs' (chapters 1–12; see 12:37), also marked the beginning of Christ's passion. Because many Jews came to believe in Jesus as a result of the miracle (11:45; 12:11), the chief priests conspired to put him (as well as Lazarus) to death.

In early English literature, Lazarus is featured in various lives of Christ (e.g., *The Stanzaic Life of Christ* [MS BM Add 39996], 1586–1763). The anonymous *Meditations on the Life and Passion of Christ* (Early English Text Society old series 158, 209–52) contain an impressive rendering of the raising as a battle between Christ and Satan. Christ's command 'Come out' is repeated over and over as a 'word of batayle'.

The miracle was dramatized in Latin by Hilarius – possibly an Englishman – in the 12th century. Later versions, usually in connection with the 'Conversion of St Mary Magdalen' (generally assumed, in the Middle Ages, to be one and the same with Mary of Bethany), are found in the Latin playbook of Fleury, France, and in the *Carmina Burana* of Benediktbeuren, Germany (in both Latin and Middle High German). English versions begin with the closely scriptural rendering of the miracle in the Chester cycle (1328), and thereafter in the York, Wakefield, and Coventry cycles, all of which adhere to the scriptural account. The Digby Play of *Mary Magdalen* (1402), which includes a 'Resuscitation of Lazarus', reflects the growth of extracanonical legend surrounding the persons of Lazarus and Mary Magdalen (as does the *Golden Legend*).

In the 17th century Francis Quarles recurs to traditional typology in his poem 'Why dost thou shade thy lovely face?' The poet asks God to redeem him like Lazarus: 'If I am dead, Lord, set death's prisoner free.' Milton, in his comments on bodily death, used John 11:13 to argue for the unorthodox view that in death the human soul is not separated from one's body, but sleeps the sleep of death (*De Doctrina Christiana*, 1.13). Blake makes symbolic use of the miracle in his poem *Milton* (1.24.26–33), where, according to S. Damon (*A Blake Dictionary*, 1965, 224), Lazarus 'represents the physical bodies of all mankind' and the resurrection becomes 'part of the false doctrine of the church' because it is understood to happen to the physical (not spiritual) body.

The question 'Where wert thou, brother, those four days?' is asked by Mary and the neighbours in Alfred Lord Tennyson's 'In Memoriam A.H.H.' (section 23). 'There lives no record of reply', and the question is submerged in the disciples' joy. Christ's humanity, as demonstrated by his weeping, is one of the topics of Elizabeth Barrett Browning's sonnet 'The Two Sayings', and of John Keble's poem 'Fill High the Bowl', which meditates on Christ's agony.

Increasing theological scepticism in the 19th century prompted a variety of revisionist readings of the miracle. In Robert Browning's 'An Epistle Containing the Strange Medical Experience of Karshish, the Arab Physician', the raising of Lazarus and his state of mind at the age of fifty, years after Christ's death, is the object of sceptical scrutiny. For Karshish. ''Tis but a case of mania – subinduced / By epilepsy, at the turning point / Of trance prolonged unduly some three days', and he sees Lazarus as divided between eternal and temporal existence. Doubts about the authenticity of the miracle are expressed indirectly by a bible-versed messenger boy in Dickens' *Our Mutual Friend*. He takes up the traditional high evaluation of the miracle in his report about the state of a drowned man: 'If Lazarus was only half as far gone, that was the greatest of all the miracles' (chapter 3). In *David Copperfield* the protagonist's mother reads to him the story of Lazarus being raised, which frightens him so that his mother and the servant are afterwards 'obliged to take me out of bed, and show me the quiet churchyard out of the bedroom window, with the dead all lying in their graves at rest, below the solemn moon' (chapter 2).

In 'Lady Lazarus' Sylvia Plath fuses the experience of her earlier attempt at suicide with a criticism of the public's sensationalistic, dehumanized interest in the disclosures after the Nazi holocaust. *Lazarus was a Lady*, a drama by John Ford Noonan, is about a young woman who uses her terminal illness as a means of manipulation. Thom Gunn's poem 'Lazarus Not Raised' describes the futility of merely human efforts to conquer death.

In Melville's *Moby Dick*, Ishmael, making his will, observes that his future days will be 'as good as the days that Lazarus lived after his resurrection; a supplementary clean gain of so many months or weeks as the case might be'. This businesslike assessment of the value of life is consistent with the whole chapter (49) – if not the whole book – in which the universe is taken to be a 'vast practical joke'. The same detachment can be found in Mark Twain, who refers ironically to the legal implications of Lazarus' resurrection. In 'The Second Advent' and 'The Holy Children', he ridicules 'special providences' and claims that a modern-day resurrection would raise disputes over the dead man's property.

'Lazarus', by Edwin Arlington Robinson, is a modern psychological study of the reactions of the sisters and Lazarus after Christ has left Bethany. The sisters want to have 'all as it was before', but having lost the security of the tomb, Lazarus has become a homeless, brooding man who wonders why he has been resurrected and asserts that 'there is worse than death'. Other modern renderings take up the same theme: for example, Alain Absire's *Lazarus* (English translation Barbara Bray), in which the protagonist, reeking of 'damp earth and rancid oils', longs for the death which has been denied to him. The Lazarus in W.B. Yeats' one-act play *Calvary* is a death-hungry character who accuses Christ of having resurrected him against his will, of having dragged him to the light 'as boys drag out / A rabbit when they have dug its hole away'. He cannot find a tomb again and demands Christ's own death: 'You took my death, give me your death instead.'

In Eugene O'Neill's drama *Lazarus Laughed*, the protagonist, after having been raised by Jesus, begins to laugh 'in the laughter of God' and answers 'There is no death' when he is asked the familiar question about his experiences beyond death. His house becomes known as the 'House of Laughter', and laughter is Lazarus' final comment on all adversities – even when members of his family are slain by Roman soldiers in a Jewish uproar against the new sect of his followers. Lazarus and his wife Miriam are taken to Athens, where he is hailed as a reincarnation of the god Dionysus, and then on to Rome. Here, too, his doctrines fascinate people, but also entangle them in a maze of love, hate, frenzy, and killing. Finally, Lazarus (who has become a young man again whereas Miriam has grown old) is executed at the stake; his last words are, 'There is no death!' The drama is less concerned with the proclamation of Christ's power over death than with a portrayal of Nietzsche's ideas of the Dionysian mode of life, of the Superman, and of the eternal return. In the end, Lazarus' soul flies 'back into the womb of Infinity' (4.2). A different and more cynical kind of laughter is reflected in Joyce's debunking reference in *Ulysses*, where Leopold Bloom, pondering the resurrection of the dead, puns on John 11:43: 'Come forth, Lazarus! And he came fifth and lost the job.'

Manfred Siebald
*Johannes Gutenberg Universität, Mainz, Germany*

## Mary Magdalene

Mary Magdalene, mentioned by Luke (8:2) as 'a certain woman which had been healed of evil spirits and infirmities… out of whom went seven devils', is listed (Mark 15:40–41) among the women who followed Jesus and ministered to him. She was at the cross (Matthew 27:56; Mark 15:40; John 19:25) and watched Joseph of Arimathea bury Jesus (Mark 15:42–47). On Easter morning she came with other women to anoint Christ's body at the tomb; they were met by angels and sent to tell the apostles of the resurrection (Matthew 27:61; 28:1–10; Mark 16:1–8; Luke 23:55 – 24:11; John 20:1–2). Mark mentions that the risen Christ 'appeared to Mary Magdalene' (16:9–11), an account amplified by John (20:11–18).

The Latin Fathers followed Tertullian (*De pudicitia*, 11.2) in combining the account of Mary Magdalene with that of the sinner who washed Christ's feet with her tears and wiped them with her hair (Luke 7:37–50). Because there is another gospel account of an anointing, this time of Christ's head by Mary of Bethany (Matthew 26:6–13; Mark 14:3–9; John 12:1–8), the identities of Mary of Bethany and Mary Magdalene could be readily merged, as they were by St Gregory the Great (*Homily*, 25.1.10). This provided Mary Magdalene with a sister and a brother (Martha and Lazarus), made Jesus a frequent visitor in her home, connected her with the contemplative life because of Jesus' comment that she had chosen 'the better part' (Luke 10:38–42), and involved her in the story of the raising of Lazarus (John 11).

Origen (in his commentary on Matthew) and the Greek Fathers who followed him insisted on three separate Marys. Origen, however, inadvertently promoted Magdalene as a symbol of erotic asceticism by comparing the perfume of the anointing of Christ to the perfume of the bride in his commentaries on the Song of Solomon (1:12–13). St Bernard of Clairvaux, for example, preached eighty-six sermons on the Song, allegorically identifying the bride with the church, the soul, the Virgin Mary, and Mary Magdalene (Sermon, 7:6).

The controversy over the identification of the three Marys is exceedingly complex, but the identification of Mary Magdalene with Mary of Bethany and with the sinful woman of Luke 7 is the basis of Western iconographical representation of Mary in literature and art, and it was never seriously challenged until Jacques Lefèvre attacked the Magdalene cult in 1516.

The Reformation effectively ended the cult of the Magdalene when Calvin separated the three Marys, devaluing Mary Magdalene as a symbol of the contemplative life. Stripped of the Provençal accretions, her story was Protestantized: Lewis Wager turns her story into a play about justification by faith in *The Life and Repentaunce of Marie Magdalene* (1567); a 1595 sermon by Nicholas Breton on John 20 uses Mary as an example of divine love, proper humility, and repentance ('Marie Magdalen's Love, upon the Twentieth Chapter of John'); in *Good News for the Vilest of Men* John Bunyan cites Mary Magdalene as proof that true repentance brings forgiveness; Lancelot Andrewes, in his 1620 Easter sermon on John 20, quotes Pseudo-Origen and Augustine on her significance as an example of faith.

Mary remained a favourite saint of Catholics during the Counter-Reformation. Robert Southwell wrote 'Mary Magdalen's Blush' about her shame for her sins and 'Mary Magdalen's Complaint at Christes Death' (see also his prose treatise, *Marie Magdalen's Funeral Teares*, 1591). The most famous English poem about her is Richard Crashaw's 'Saint Mary Magdalene; or, the Weeper', full of extended conceits, capturing the entire story of the anointing in the phrase 'What prince's wanton'est pride e'er could / Wash with silver, wipe with gold?' Andrew Marvell is heavily influenced by Crashaw in his

'Eyes and Tears', adding the striking simile of Magdalene's tears as 'liquid chaines' which flowed 'to fetter her Redeemer's feet'. Thomas Robinson, in *The Life and Death of Mary Magdalene* (circa 1620), emphasizes a lush, sensuous description of the lovers in the garden and of the palace of pleasure; after Mary's repentance he uses descriptions from the Song of Solomon to describe Christ. *St Marie Magdalen's Conversion* (anonymous 1603) uses the form of the epyllion to show the conquest of divine love over base passion as she seeks forgiveness.

Mary Magdalene was not totally rejected by Protestant poets in the early 17th century. Robert Herrick in the quatrain 'Upon Woman and Mary' concludes that Christ first called her 'Woman' when her faith was small, 'Mary' when she believed. George Herbert in 'Marie Magdalene' focuses on a paradox of the anointing: 'She being stain'd her self, why did she strive / To make him clean, who could not be defil'd?' John Donne compliments a patron in 'To the Lady Magdalen Herbert, of St Mary Magdalen', mentioning her holdings in Bethina and Magdalo, the resurrection appearance, and the controversy over the number of Marys, concluding with an admonition to the lady to copy the latter half of Mary's life.

By the late 17th century the Magdalene is frequently referred to in jest. In Richard Brome's play *The Damoiselle* a comic character named Mrs Magdalen is drunk: 'She's in her Mawdlin fit; all her wine / Showres out in tears.' She is rarely mentioned in the 18th century, save in such ironic allusions as Alexander Pope's Epistle 2, 'To a Lady: On the Character of Women', where a reference to 'Magdalen's loose hair and lifted eye' serves as a transition between 'naked Leda' and 'sweet St Cecilia'.

Magdalene as a prostitute re-enters English literature with William Blake, who suggests in 'The Everlasting Gospel' that if Jesus wanted to take on the sins of the world, his mother should have been 'an Harlot... Just such a one as Magdalen with seven devils'. A character in Shaw's play *Good King Charles' Golden Days* who claims, 'Nell is no worse than Mary Magdalene', is told by a proper matron, 'I hope Mary Magdalen made a good end and was forgiven... But I should not have asked her into my house' (act 1). The name Magdalene becomes a noun, indicating a repentant prostitute or an unwed mother. In *Man and Superman* Shaw argues that morality makes 'a weeping Magdalen and an innocent child branded with shame' (act 1), exactly the situation portrayed by Wordsworth in *The Excursion* when the wanderer finds 'a weeping Magdalene' by her baby's grave (6.814). Both Dylan Thomas ('The Countryman's Return,' 85) and James Joyce (*Finnegans Wake*) later use the name in this sense, as does Hugh Blunt in his compilation of lives of reformed prostitutes, *The Great Magdalens* (1928). Paintings of the Magdalene are sometimes the subject of poetry; Wordsworth describes 'the painted Magdalen of Le Brun... pale and bedropped with everflowing tears' (*The Prelude*, 3.76–80), Byron compares a sorrowful woman to 'The Magdalen of Guido', and Browning writes about 'Bold Castelfranco's Magdalen', penitent in her rock den.

The 20th century has seen a resurgence of dramatic interest in Mary Magdalene. In Paul Heyse's German drama *Mary of Magdala* she is placed in the dilemma of being able to save Jesus by giving herself to a Roman; Maurice Maeterlinck's *Mary Magdalene* is heavily indebted to Heyse. She is the focus of John Peale Bishop's *The Funeral of St Mary Magdalene*, Florence Evans' *Mary Magdalen*, John Nicholson's *The Sainted Courtezan*, and Fernando Mota's *Maria de Magdala*, as well as of numerous plays written for religious instruction. Dorothy L. Sayers' radio dramas *The Man Born to Be King* follow medieval precedents in equating the three Marys, in giving Mary poetical lamentations, and in citing Mary's desire to kiss Jesus' feet as his body is being anointed. More recently, Mary Magdalene has played a role almost as important as Jesus in the American musicals *Jesus Christ Superstar* and *Godspell*.

Mary appears more often as a symbol of eroticism than asceticism in modern fiction. In *The Last Temptation of Christ* by Nikos Kazantzakis, she constitutes Christ's final test, symbolizing erotic love as 'the sweetest the world can offer', an offer which Christ ultimately rejects. In *Report to Greco* Mary possesses life-giving power, resurrecting the Christ; however, in 'The Man Who Died' D.H. Lawrence reverses that role when Jesus specifically rejects Mary and all others who want him to be God. Leopold Bruckberger has written a 'biography' of her life, *Marie Madeleine: soror mea sponsa*, emphasizing the erotic asceticism with references to the Song of Solomon, and William E.

Phipps, in his book *Was Jesus Married?*, concludes that Jesus married Mary Magdalene.

American poets have stressed her symbolic value. In Hart Crane's *The Bridge* the woman is asked, 'Eve! Magdalene! or Mary, you?' ('Southern Cross') and is later addressed as 'O Magdalene' ('National Winter Garden'); promiscuity and forgiveness are the themes of Louis Simpson's poem 'The Man Who Married Magdalen'. The erotic penitent reappears in Brother Antoninus' 'A Savagery of Love', a canticle for the feast of St Mary Magdalene, demonstrating the unresolved tension between the sacred and the profane which is at the heart of the legend of Magdalene, 'the Venus in sackcloth'.

Margaret Hannay
*Siena College*

## Mary, Mother of Jesus

Although Mary the mother of Jesus is of almost unrivalled importance in historic Christianity and her role in relation to salvation history is evidently central, she has a comparatively modest role in the Bible itself. Relationship between pertinent New Testament narratives and later elaborate growth of the cultus of the Virgin, a rich and complex study, may be but scantly apprehended in a sketch of literary developments alone. The actual appearances of Mary in the New Testament narrative include Gabriel's annunciation of her election as mother of the Messiah (Luke 1:26–38), Mary's visit to her cousin Elisabeth (Luke 1:39–56), the journey to Bethlehem and the nativity (Luke 2:1–20), the presentation of Jesus at the Temple to Simeon and Anna (Luke 2:21–39), Mary's anxious discovery (with Joseph) of twelve-year-old Jesus discoursing with the elders (Luke 2:40–52), her intervention with Jesus on behalf of the wine stewards at the marriage of Cana (John 2:1–11), her visit to Jesus with his 'brothers' (Matthew 12:46; Mark 3:31–35; Luke 8:19–21), her place at the foot of the cross with John, there to hear her son's last words to her (John 19:26–27), and her presence with the apostles at Pentecost (Acts 1:14). Yet in many of these narrative pericopes her appearances are cameo, and in several she is not accorded speech. The evangelists' reasons for seemingly spartan restraint in the treatment of Mary have

61

prompted considerable theological reflection. Moreover, the silence in the biblical texts has invited manifold speculation, including apocryphal writings. Out of these, too, have evolved certain teachings of the Roman Catholic Church, which in their turn have become also the subject of literary allusion.

The central importance of Mary in Christian tradition and literature, however, is strictly biblical – her role as 'mother of Jesus' or, in Elisabeth's words, 'mother of my Lord' (Luke 1:43). Related to this is Mary's reference to herself in Luke's Gospel as 'handmaiden of the Lord' (Luke 1:38, 48). In this regard Mary is presented in the New Testament as the instrument of divine grace whereby the awesome and unapproachable holiness of God condescends to be conjoined to the frailty and impermanence of fallen humanity: the centrality of the incarnation to all Christian teaching about Jesus makes Mary, as the chosen vessel, the immediate focus of God's redeeming love for the world. Much in the manner of Old Testament figures like Enoch (Genesis 5:22) and Noah (who 'found grace in the eyes of the Lord', Genesis 6:8), Mary is 'highly favoured' with God (Luke 1:28, 30) and particularly 'blessed... among women' (28, 42), a blessing Mary herself recognizes explicitly in her *Magnificat* (Luke 1:46–55) as a fulfilment of God's covenant love and promise. It is evident that early associations of Jesus' conception and birth with Old Testament messianic prophecies include notably Mary's unprecedented virgin conception (cf. Luke 1:34). The promise in Isaiah – 'Behold, a virgin shall conceive, and bear a son, and shall call his name Immanuel' (7:14) – is explicitly brought to bear in Matthew's nativity narrative (1:22–23). In this way, the virginity of Mary became one of the crucial tokens for early believers that Jesus was 'the Christ' long expected, and thus a central tenet of basic Christology.

Mary appears regularly in Old English literature. Yet it is not until the 13th century that literary tributes in English to Mary really begin to flourish. Franciscan devotion to Mary in particular was expressed in scores of lyrics and carols. Latin hymns such as the '*Stabat Iuxta Christi Crucem*' and the '*Mater Salutaris*' were translated into the vernacular ('at leueli leor wid spald ischent' and numerous poems began to appear on Marian subjects.

Prayer to the Virgin is the prime reason for a large percentage of vernacular English lyrics and carols, and even so strict a biblicist as John Wyclif thought it 'impossible that we should obtain the reward of heaven without the help of Mary. There is no sex or age,' he continues, 'no rank or position of anyone in the human race which has no need to call upon the help of the Holy Virgin' (Sermones, 1.200, ed. Lechler). Chaucer accords to his Second Nun's prologue her eloquent devotion to the Virgin, and his 'Prière a Nostre Dame' (or 'ABC of Our Lady') is an alphabetic 84-line penitential appeal, incorporating much of the traditional typology (as also does Lydgate's 'Queen of Heaven, of Hell eke Empresse'). Like Wyclif, however, Chaucer steers clear of the more extravagant noncanonical legends. In Chaucer's Prioress' Tale, a sentimental and anti-Semitic melodrama in which the putative child-martyr sings the alma redemptoris mater even after his murder, Chaucer seems to satirize misfocused piety.

Perhaps if England had been more influenced by Wyclif and Luther than by Calvin and Cromwell, even Reformation poets might have shied away less sharply from Mary as a subject for poetry. Calvin's central contention that Mary's 'virtues and all her excellences are nothing other than the generosity of God' (New Testament Commentaries, 1.22) leads him to insist that it 'is quite absurd to teach that we are to seek from her anything which she receives otherwise than we do ourselves' (cf. a similar formulation in St Thomas Aquinas, Summa Theologica, 3.2.2.3). Calvin consistently resists the parallel veneration of Mary 'which has resulted in Christ being shoved down the bench, so to say, while Mary is given the place of honour' (New Testament Commentaries, 1.32–33). Yet he adds: 'To this day we cannot enjoy the blessing brought to us in Christ without thinking at the same time of that which God gave as adornment and honour to Mary, in willing her to be the mother of his only-begotten Son' (32). The iconoclasm which denigrated Mary and largely banished her from English literature after the 1540s especially is more extreme. Crowning the general iconoclasm was secularizing appropriation by Elizabeth I, the 'Virgin Queen', of many traditional Marian symbols (rose, star, moon, etc.). Thus, though in Anglican worship Mary was not excluded (the Magnificat continued to be recited each day at

Evensong), Protestant poets of the 16th and 17th centuries have less to say about Mary. In all the religious poetry of George Herbert, for example, she is mentioned only in a two-line anagram 'Mary / Army': 'How well her name an *Army* doth present / In whom the Lord of Hosts did pitch his tent!' Milton's Mary is that of the canonical Bible. In *Paradise Regained* Milton builds up a sense of her role in the narrative by having her recount the chief events of her (canonical) life since the annunciation, giving content to the scriptural notation 'And Mary kept all these things and pondered them in her heart' (*Paradise Regained* 2.60–108). But postbiblical doctrines of the Catholic Church are all absent from his text.

The 18th century, with its tension-filled religious controversy and general hostility to any suspicion of 'Papism' (Jesuit spirituality in particular) made little in the way of additional contribution to the literature. Even Catholic poets (e.g., Alexander Pope) eschew the subject. If by the beginning of the 19th century there is a sea change, it owes in part to the same spirit of liberalism which agitated for the Roman Catholic Relief Act of 1829. Sir Walter Scott's '*Ave Maria!* Maiden mild!' in canto 3 of his *Lady of the Lake*, and William Wordsworth's 'The Virgin' (*Ecclesiastical Sonnets*, 2.25) are celebrations of ideal human nature, though each makes an explicit effort to recognize traditional Catholic teaching. In Wordsworth's poem the immaculate conception is suggested:

> Mother! Whose virgin bosom was uncrost
> With the least shade of thought to sin allied;
> Woman! Above all women glorified,
> Our tainted nature's solitary boast...

Coleridge's younger cousin Mary Coleridge (1861–1907) treats Mary's representative role in such a way as to create a more radical political statement:

> Mother of God! no lady thou:
> Common woman of common earth!
> Our Lady ladies call thee now,
> But Christ was never of gentle birth;
> A common man of the common earth.

For God's ways are not as our ways.
The noblest lady in the land
Would have given up half her days,
Would have cut off her right hand
To bear the Child that was God of the land…

And still for men to come she sings,
Nor shall her singing pass away.
*'He hath filled the hungry with good things'* –
O listen, lords and ladies gay! –
*'And the rich He hath sent empty away.'*

After the conversion of John Henry (Cardinal) Newman in 1845, the effect of the Oxford Movement among Anglicans and in English culture generally produced a signal recrudescence of interest in Mary. Much of this, and some of the best writing, came from new converts, for example, Eric Gill, Lionel Johnson, G.K. Chesterton, and Gerard Manley Hopkins. Newman's close friend (and fellow priest of the Church of England) Edward Caswall translated Marian hymns and produced also a volume of poetry entitled *The Masque of Mary and Other Poems* shortly after his conversion to Catholicism in 1847.

Catholic-born Oscar Wilde, though not religious in practice through much of his life, wrote traditional orisons to Mary ('San Miniato'; '*Ave Maria Gratia Plena*'). And from the pre-Raphaelite movement issued romanticized evocations of Mary's 'ponderings' such as Dante Gabriel Rossetti's 'Mary's Girlhood' (cf. his '*Ave*'):

This is the blesséd Mary, pre-elect
God's virgin. Gone is a great while, and she
Dwelt young in Nazareth of Galilee.

Unto God's will she brought devout respect
Profound simplicity of intellect.
And supreme patience. From her mother's knee
Faithful and hopeful; wise in charity;
Strong in grave peace; in pity circumspect.

So held she through her girlhood; as it were
  An angel-watered lily, that near God
  Grows and is quiet. Till, one day at home
She woke in her white bed, and had no fear
  At all – yet wept till sunshine, and felt awed:
  Because the fulness of the time was come.

Sublimation of Mary in 19th-century fiction would seem to account for female figures such as the Madonna figure in George Eliot's novel *Romola* (cf. Dickens' Ada in *Bleak House* and Amy in *Little Dorrit*). More telling, perhaps, is the explanation Ruskin gives to romantic nostalgia for her former place in the European mythos. Writing in his *Fors Clavigera* (letter 41; cf. *Stones of Venice*, 2.3.39–40) Ruskin says:

> To the common Protestant mind the dignities ascribed to the Madonna have been always a violent offence; they are one of the parts of the Catholic faith which are openest to reasonable dispute, and least comprehensible by the average realistic and materialist temper of the Reformation.
>
> But after the most careful examination, neither as adversary nor as friend, of the influences of Catholicism for good and evil, I am persuaded that the worship of the Madonna has been one of its noblest and most vital graces, and has never been otherwise than productive of true holiness of life and purity of character. I do not enter into any question as to the truth or fallacy of the idea; I no more wish to defend the historical or theological position of the Madonna than that of St Michael or St Christopher; but I am certain that to the habit of reverent belief in, and contemplation of, the character ascribed to the heavenly hierarchies, we must ascribe the highest results yet achieved in human nature.

In the 20th century the theme of a modern Mary bearing a divine child, or one believed by the mother and others to have been miraculously conceived, is almost tediously common. A prominent example is John Barth's *Giles Goat-Boy, or, The Revised New Syllabus* (1966) in which the hero's mother, Miss Virginia Hector, who repeatedly assures people that she has never 'gone all the way' with anyone, is seduced and raped by a giant computer. To escape the persecution of the chancellor of the university, who, Herod-like, wishes the child destroyed, Virginia takes him away to raise him, disguised as a goat, on the college agricultural station (the goat is a parody of the Lamb of God). Those modern retellings of Gospel narrative that follow the Gospel fairly closely do least with their Mary figures (e.g., B.P. Galdos, *Nazarin*, 1895; Antonio Fogazzaro, *The Saint*, 1905; Elizabeth S. Phelps Ward, *A Singular Life*, 1895; Elizabeth Linton, *Joshua Davidson*, 1872). It has been noted that for modern fiction writers Mary 'is an awkward figure to deal with. If she is present in a modern transfiguration, then realism will not permit her to be a virgin; but if she is not a virgin then she is no longer the venerated object of cultic adoration. It is much simpler to ignore her. In the Marxist-oriented novels there is no mother figure at all'. Yet faded memory, if not nostalgia, is a prerequisite for popular diabolical parallels such as the cinematic *Rosemary's Baby*.

Perhaps the best traditional poem on Mary published in the 20th century (1918; written in the 1870s) remains Hopkins' '*Rosa Mystica*'. A poem expressing at once both evident devotion and great restraint, it probes the mystery of a traditional element in her typology and iconography (the 'rose' of the Song of Solomon) as a way of re-establishing the meaning of the biblical Mary and her role in the divine plan of salvation:

> Is Mary the rose, then? Mary the tree?
> But the blossom, the blossom there, who can it be? –
> Who can her rose be? It could be but one:
> Christ Jesus, our Lord, her God and her son.
> *In the gardens of God, in the daylight divine*
> *Shew me thy son, mother, mother of mine.*

Among the most important modern collections of poems centred on Mary is *Pieta* (1966) by R.S. Thomas, a rector in the Church of Wales, also of a strikingly traditional character.

David L. Jeffrey
*University of Ottawa*

## Nicodemus

Nicodemus was a Pharisee and a member of the Sanhedrin, 'a ruler of the Jews' whose profound if covert late-night conversation with Jesus is a key narrative in the Gospel of John (chapter 3). He also appears on two further occasions. When Jesus proclaimed himself in the Temple to be the source of 'living water', Nicodemus intervened against those Pharisees who wished to censure him, and was rebuffed for doing so (John 7:50–52). He re-enters the narrative at the burial of Jesus (John 19:38–42) when, with Joseph of Arimathea, another member of the Sanhedrin who had become a supporter of Jesus, he prepared the body for entombment in the sepulchre.

The first narrative represents the situation of thoughtful religious Jews, intent on the law but figuratively still 'in the dark' concerning the nature of the spiritual 'kingdom' spoken of by Jesus. Leaders such as Nicodemus yearned for a political messiah who would deliver their people from Roman oppression; to many, Jesus' teaching was therefore not only perplexing but suspect or even anathema. Nicodemus nonetheless honoured Jesus with the title 'Rabbi' and acknowledged him as a 'teacher sent from God' (3:2), inviting further explanation of the 'kingdom within'. In his reply, Jesus spoke of the need for being 'born again of water and the Spirit' (3:5), suggesting the primary need for repentance and inward renewal. At first Nicodemus did not understand Jesus' figurative language: can one 'enter the second time into his mother's womb, and be born?' he asks incredulously. After hearing Jesus speak of the difference between the invisible direction of God's Spirit and the carnal motivations of the flesh ('That which is born of the flesh is flesh; and that which is born of the spirit is spirit. Marvel not that I said unto thee, Ye must be born again' (3:6–7), Nicodemus exclaims in frustration: 'How can these things be?' Jesus chides him gently for his literal-mindedness: 'Art thou a master of Israel and knowest not these things?' (3:10), thereby indicating the congruence of his message (and metaphor) with that of the 'law and the prophets' in which Nicodemus was in some sense expert.

The 4th-century *Acta Pilati* and the *Descensus Christi ad infernos* were foundational to the creation of the so-called Gospel of Nicodemus, widely popular by the 14th century for its narration of the Harrowing of Hell. The text is partially translated in the English *Cursor Mundi* (circa AD1300), which refers to Nicodemus throughout the Gospel paraphrase as 'Sire Nicodemus', the 'frend' of Jesus and his 'knight'. Referring to the events in John 19:38–42, the text ascribes Nicodemus' 'book' to his difficulty in persuading his fellow Jews of his own hard-won convictions about Jesus (3.17277–88). The apocryphal Gospel to which Nicodemus' name is attached had considerable influence upon English medieval literature, including, notably, the Towneley cycle play 'The Deliverance of Souls' and the 'harrowing' analogue in *Piers Plowman* (B.18.262, 316a–17).

If Nicodemus fared somewhat less well in English literature after the Reformation it may have been in large part due to the Reformation theologians' impatience with apocryphal texts. Another factor may have been Calvin's harsh and unsympathetic reading of Nicodemus' interview with Jesus (e.g., 'Nicodemus rejects [Jesus' words] as a fable'; 'Because Christ sees that He is wasting his time and energy in teaching this proud man, He now rebukes him' [*New Testament Commentary*, 4.60–61, 69, 203–04]). Nevertheless, a more sympathetic view persists. John Donne's sermon on 'John 22:21' accords with the Middle English *Ancrene Riwle* in seeing Nicodemus in John 19:39 as a dramatic symbol of penance, and Henry Vaughan's 'The Night' reflects his reading of Augustine's commentary throughout:

> …Wise Nicodemus saw such light
> As made him know his God by night.
> Most blest believer he!
> Who in that land of darkness and blinde eyes
> Thy long expected healing wings could see,
> When thou didst rise,
> And what can never more be done,
> Did at mid-night speak with the Sun!

Matthew Henry (1728) departs markedly from Calvin in his commentary: 'Not many mighty and noble are called; yet some are, and here was one… this was a man of the Pharisees, bred to learning, a scholar' (*Commentary on the Whole Bible*, 5.88); of the encounter Henry goes on to say: 'These were *Noctes Christianae* – *Christian nights*, much more instructive than the *Noctes Atticae – Attic nights'*, and of Jesus' 'answer' he draws a general application:

> This is a reproof (1) To those who undertake to teach others and yet are ignorant and unskilful in the word of righteousness themselves. (2) To those who spend their time in learning and teaching notions and ceremonies in religion, niceties and criticisms in the Scripture, and neglect that which is practical and tends to reform the heart and life. (885)

Henry defends Nicodemus against the blame of some Christian commentators (including Calvin) that Nicodemus yet 'retained his place in the council and his vote among them', and observes rather that Christ 'never said to him *Follow me*... therefore it seems rather to have been his *wisdom* not immediately to throw up his place'. Most praiseworthy for Henry, however, is Nicodemus' later public defence of Jesus and equally visible participation in the burial of his body: 'Let none justify the disguising of their faith by the example of Nicodemus, unless, like him, they be ready upon the first occasion openly to appear in the cause of Christ, though they stand alone in it; for so Nicodemus did here, and ch. xix.39' (5.978).

Matthew Henry notwithstanding, Nicodemus seems to have attracted little interest in 18th-century literature. In Dickens' *Our Mutual Friend* there may be a recollection when at the return of John Harmon from the 'dead' Nicodemus Boffin wakes up and asks a series of apt questions. A spate of 20th-century dramatizations reflect the importance of John 3 in evangelical preaching, including Katherine Lee Bates' *Pharisees* (1926), in which Nicodemus and a rabbi are the chief characters; P.E. Osgood's *The Fears of Nicodemus* (1928), a dramatic sermon dialogue between Nicodemus and Joseph of Arimathea; and Perry J. Stackhouse's *The Disciple of the Night* (1926), also designed as an aid to preaching. The title poem of Edwin Arlington Robinson's collection *Nicodemus* (1932) features a dramatic dialogue between Nicodemus and Caiaphas, at whose bidding Nicodemus has evidently interviewed Jesus secretly. The poem is about fear of the unknown, and 'flawed complacency'. When Caiaphas finds that Nicodemus has been swayed by 'the carpenter' he is gently – but also menacingly – reproving, refusing Nicodemus' request that he join his colleague, 'but once, to see and hear him, Caiaphas'. Sholem Asch's novel *The Nazarene* (1939) alternates between the 1st and 20th centuries in its view of the life of Yeshua; Nicodemon figures prominently as a faithful rabbi. Perhaps the most penetrating modern literary representation is that of the American poet Howard Nemerov, which amplifies the questions of Nicodemus artfully; in the final section of his poem 'Nicodemus', Nemerov shows close familiarity with the exposition of St Augustine to his catechumens (*In Joannis Evangelium Tractatus*, especially 11.7–13) a millennium and a half earlier, but represents Nicodemus' final response to Jesus' invitation to the new birth in terms rather of a request to reiterate the exodus deliverance and the covenant promise to Abraham.

David L. Jeffrey
*University of Ottawa*

## Peter

St Peter, foremost among the disciples and, with St Paul, most prominent of the apostles after Pentecost, is one of the most colourful and complex of New Testament characters. He has traditionally been credited with two contributions to the New Testament canon, the Epistles of 1 and 2 Peter. Because he is so often a foil for Jesus, the signal events of his life closely parallel the main events in the ministry and proclamation of Jesus. After the ascension, as leader of the young church in Jerusalem, later at Antioch, and then in Rome, he fulfilled the role assigned to him by Jesus as a foundation for the church. Roman bishops have been chief among bishops in the Western church since Linus, Anencletus, and Clement I, Peter's first successors in Rome, although the title 'Pope' (Greek *pappas*; Latin *papa*) did not come to be associated exclusively with the Roman bishop until after the 5th century.

Born in Bethsaida (probably at the north end of Lake Gennesaret), the town also of St Philip, Peter was a brother of St Andrew. Their father's name was Jonah (Matthew 16:7; John 1:42) – the notion that Bar-Jona means 'anarchist' or 'zealot' is fictional. After Peter's marriage he settled in Capernaum, where he was living in the home of his mother-in-law (Matthew 8:14; Mark 1:30; Luke 4:38) at the beginning of the public ministry of Jesus. According to St Clement of Alexandria (Stromateis, 3.6), he had children, and that his wife accompanied him on at least some of his missionary tours is suggested by the fact that she was known at Corinth (1 Corinthians 9:5). Clement indicates that at some later point she, like her husband, suffered martyrdom (Stromateis, 7.9). While in Capernaum Peter plied his trade as a fisherman, and owned his own boat (Luke 5:1–11). He and Andrew had been attracted there to the penitential preaching of John the Baptist (John 1:40–42).

The statement in Acts 4:13 that Peter and John were 'unlearned and ignorant men' probably ought not to be taken too extremely; the phrase may mean merely that they lacked recourse to rabbinical training in the Torah and its interpretation. On the other hand, Peter is always presented in the New Testament as rough and ready, earnest yet volatile, desirous of spiritual good yet neither disciplined in his thought nor meditative.

Several of the key narratives concerning Peter in all four Gospels underline Peter's human fallibility, but the most emphatic representation of his weaknesses comes in Mark's account (which has been thought to derive directly from Peter's own recollections as related to the author). Like John and the other Synoptics, Mark ranks Peter as first of the disciples and chief spokesperson for the Twelve, but he also singles him out for blame at critical points in the narrative. It is Peter who leads the group to Jesus and tries to press on him the role of popular teacher (1:35–37). At Caesarea Philippi (8:27–33) Jesus hears Peter's confession that he is the Messiah with some reserve, and when Peter rebukes Jesus for saying that 'the Son of man must suffer many things, and be rejected... and be killed, and after three days rise again', Jesus reprimands Peter in turn, saying, 'Get thee behind me, Satan: for thou savourest not the things that be of God, but the things that be of men' (8:33). At the transfiguration Peter's suggestion that three 'tabernacles' be set up to honour Moses, Elijah, and Jesus appears to have been an utterance of nervous foolishness, the narrative adding, 'For he wist not what to say, for they were sore afraid' (9:6). He is singled out for reproach for falling asleep while he should be praying in Gethsemane (14:37), and his famous three denials of Jesus after the capture (14:66–72) are recounted in such a way as to create the suspicion that he may even have 'cursed' his Lord (14:71), a cardinal offence in the early church (1 Corinthians 12:3). Yet for all that, the resurrected Jesus sends with the angel at the tomb a special message to Peter (16:7).

The accounts of Matthew, Luke, and John in various ways soften the notice of these failings, balancing the frailty of Peter, as exhibited in his lapse of faith after his bold request to walk to Jesus on the water, with an emphasis on his learning to depend absolutely on his Lord rather than acting unreflectingly merely on his own strength (Matthew 14:23–33). Also, at the confession incident, Matthew includes Jesus' response to Peter's recognition of his Messiahship which, even as it points to Peter's mortal limitations, makes the famous pun on his name (Aramaic *Kepha'* > *Kephas*; Greek *Petros/Petra*; Latin *Petrus/Petrum*) the introduction to an unmatched special calling of Peter to apostolic leadership in the church:

> Blessed art thou, Simon Bar-jona: for flesh and blood hath not revealed it to thee, but my father which is in heaven. And I say also unto thee, That thou art Peter, and upon this rock I will build my church; and the gates of hell shall not prevail against it. And I will give unto thee the keys of the kingdom of heaven: and whatsoever thou shalt bind on earth shall be bound in heaven: and whatsoever thou shalt loose on earth shall be loosed in heaven. (Matthew 16:17–19)

This call to apostleship was renewed following Peter's denials and the events surrounding Calvary and the tomb, when Jesus met Peter and some of the other disciples after they fished in vain all night. From the shore, unrecognized, Jesus urged Peter to cast his net again, and when he did, the catch was so great it could hardly be hauled in. The disciples (having experienced another such miraculous draught of fishes [Luke 5:4–11]) then recognized Jesus, and Peter leapt into the sea to get to shore, where Jesus already was cooking fish over a fire of charcoal. After the meal, Jesus asked Peter, 'Simon, son of Jonas, lovest thou me?' and twice received the answer, 'Yea, Lord, thou knowest that I love thee.' When Jesus asked the third time, exasperated, Peter replied emphatically, 'Lord, thou knowest all things; thou knowest that I love thee.' Then, the threefold confession having reversed the earlier threefold denial, Peter received his commission, 'Feed my sheep', along with a prophecy concerning his own martyrdom (John 21:16–19). Even on this occasion, however, Peter was chastened by Jesus for improper curiosity concerning the vocation of another of the disciples (21:21–24). Only John (18:10) among the four evangelists names Peter as the 'one standing by' at the betrayal and arrest of Jesus who struck off the ear of the servant of the high priest (and was reprimanded by Jesus for his action).

For all his shortcomings, Peter remained *primus inter pares* in the accounts of Matthew and Luke especially: he speaks for all on a number of occasions (e.g., Matthew 15:15; 19:27; Luke 12:41) and answers the Lord in their name (e.g., Matthew 16:16). In addition, there are numerous instances in which Jesus makes addresses to Peter (e.g., Matthew 26:40; Luke 22:31) or sends him on a special errand of instruction, for example, when Peter is sent to catch the fish in whose mouth is found the coin necessary to pay the tribute money (Matthew 17:24–27).

After the ascension, when the disciples and Jesus' mother Mary were met together at Pentecost, there to experience the descent of the Holy Spirit, Peter stood up to answer the mockers and, as spokesman for the community, preached a powerful sermon at which 3,000 people were converted. He was also the first to open up the Christian community to Gentile converts, in the conversion of Cornelius the Roman centurion (Acts 11:18). He became the evident leader of the Jerusalem community, in decision-making as well as in preaching (Acts 1:15–22; 2:14–40; 3:12–26). He was spokesperson before the Jewish leaders (4:5ff.). Within the fledgling Christian community he provided dynamic leadership (5:1–11), even performing miracles (5:15). His still headstrong character and tendency to focus on external matters caused him initially to insist upon Jewish observances for converts at Antioch, for which he was rebuked by Paul. (His first epistle is often adduced as evidence that he responded well to this admonishment.)

After a brief appearance at the Jerusalem Council (Acts 15:7–11) Peter vanishes from the New Testament record. It is in later sources, such as the Epistle of Clement to the Corinthians, St Irenaeus (*Adversus haereses*, 3.1.1), and Eusebius (*Historia ecclesiastica*, 2.25.8; cf. 4.14.1), that one learns of Peter and Paul's joint labours in building the church at Rome and their martyrdom there. The apocryphal Acts of St Peter and St Paul as well as Acts of St Peter adds details about Peter's crucifixion upside down, circa 67, and the dates and other details accord well with Tacitus' description of Nero's pogrom against Roman Christians in 65–68 (*Annales*, 15.44). The statement in 1 Clement 5–6 that both Peter and Paul were executed under Nero's rule has been generally accepted by historians. The feast of St Peter and St Paul was kept in Rome as early as the 3rd century on June 29.

Representation of Peter in early English literature is, at least until the 14th century, surprisingly marginal. Despite his dramatic life and prominence in the apostolic community, the most famous Old English poem on the early missionary church is *Andreas*, concentrating almost exclusively, as its title suggests, on Peter's brother Andrew. *The Fates of the Apostles* merely notes, following the tradition, that Peter, like Paul, was among those who gave their lives in Rome through Nero's cruel cunning, and that 'their apostleship is widely honoured among the nations' (14–15).

Perhaps because he is regarded as sacrosanct (or in the 14th century by reason of the papal schism indirectly controversial) Peter receives little individual development in later medieval literature. The notable exception is Langland's allegorical treatment in *Piers Plowman*, where the name Piers or Peter implies that the idealized ploughman is a 'rock', in some sense a foundation or bedrock for whatever strength the church in the world might have. He is in this poem the type of the good Christian layperson as well as priest: in book 15 (B-text) the dreamer is told that only Piers can show him charity (cf. 1 Peter 4:8) and here he is equated with Christ: '*Petrus, id est Christus*'. Throughout the poem Piers represents the apostle's ministry, resembling at various points the patriarchs, prophets, Christ, disciples, apostles, and, of course, Peter (book 19). In terms of medieval fourfold allegory he may be seen literally as a ploughman; tropologically as the good Christian layperson; allegorically as Christ's temporal church; anagogically as a figure, like Peter, for the ideal priesthood.

Reformation writers, because of their central dispute with papal authority and its appeal to foundation in the doctrine of apostolic succession, are inclined either to slight Peter somewhat, to attack the claim of Roman succession, or to try to undermine the readings typically given to certain biblical texts and especially to extra-canonical tradition. Calvin is conservative, explaining Matthew 16:18 ('Thou art Peter, and upon this rock...') in such a way that it not only refers admiringly to Peter but 'extends to all believers, each of whom is a temple of God, and compact together by faith makes up one temple'. But, he allows, 'it also marks out Peter's preeminence, as each in his own order receives more or less according to the measure of the gift of Christ' (*Harmony of the Gospels*, 2.186). He connects the 'keys' with Luke 11:52, where 'Christ says.... that the Scribes and Pharisees, as interpreters of the Law, likewise have the key of the kingdom of heaven. For we know that the gate of life is only opened to us by the Word of God.' In polemic against Roman authority in the *Institutes*, however, he argues against Peter ever having been bishop of Rome (4.6.14–17) and asserts his conviction that the 'ancient Church' did not recognize itself as unified in allegiance to Rome or to Peter, but rather to Christ (cf. 4.7.1–30). It is Calvin's position in the *Institutes* which tends to characterize Reformation and later Puritan views, so typically diminishing the prominence of Peter in literature written within a Protestant sphere of influence.

The renaming of Peter and the keys of the kingdom passage (Matthew 16:17–19) are conspicuously absent from Spenser's *Faerie Queene*, as from most major English literary texts after the Reformation. The Jesuit poet Robert Southwell has, however, a remarkable long poem, *St Peter's Complaint*, based on an Italian work by Luigi Tansillo. In it Peter describes his misery: 'I that in vaunts displayed Pride's fairest flags / Disrobed of Grace, am wrapped in Adam's rags.' The poem focuses on Peter's grief and sense of guilt after his denial of Jesus in order to develop his absolute dependence upon God's mercy, a mercy complete enough to extend even to one who has turned his back on Christ. Richard Crashaw, whose '*Umbra S. Petri Medetur Aegrotis*' is a brief meditation on Acts 5:15 in the light of apostolic succession, also wrote two similar quatrains in English (*Steps to the Temple*). The first, 'On St Peter Cutting off Malchus' Ear', addresses the apostle:

> Well, Peter, dost thou wield thy active sword;
> Well for thyself, I mean, not for thy Lord.
> To strike at ears is to take heed there be
> No witness, Peter, of thy perjury.

The second, which equally captures the apostle's sometimes self-contradictory character and the moral lesson he affords future Christians, is 'On St Peter Casting away his Nets at Our Saviour's Call':

> Thou hast the art on't, Peter, and canst tell
> To cast thy nets on all occasions well.
> When Christ calls, and thy nets would have thee stay,
> To cast them well's to cast them quite away.

In his notes on Valdesso's 'Considerations', George Herbert, like Calvin, identifies Peter with the conveyance of Scripture. Referring to the conversion of Cornelius he writes: 'There the case is plaine, *Cornelius* had revelation, yet Peter was to be sent for, and those that have inspirations still must use *Peter*, God's Word.' In Milton's *Lycidas* Peter appears in traditional guise as a model for clerical vocation. He is 'the Pilot of the *Galilean* lake. / Two massy keys he bore of metals twain, / (The Golden opes, the Iron shuts amain). / He shook his Mitred locks and stern bespake…' and Milton has him declaim words pertinent to the office of those who would feed Christ's sheep (108–31). Bunyan, like Herbert and others, notes Peter's rebuke of Simon Magus (Acts 8:19–22), but like many of his Puritan contemporaries follows the line that Peter vacillated between boasting bravery and cowardice when the chips were down:

> He would swagger, Ay he would: He would, as his vain mind prompted him to say, do better, and stand more for his Master, then all men: But who so foiled, and run down with these Villains [Faint-heart, Mistrust, and Guilt] as he?

Writers in the 18th century continue to treat Peter circumspectly, if at all. Dryden, for example, in his Catholic conversion poem *The Hind and the Panther*, avoids direct mention. Swift's ecclesiastical satire *The Tale of a Tub* pits three brothers against each other in contest for the cloak of the church, Peter (Rome), Martin (Luther, and by extension, Anglicanism), and Jack (more extreme English dissenters); but it is not the biblical character one sees in this 'Peter' so much as a caricature of the Catholic doctrines of apostolic succession and ecclesiastical authority.

Specific incidents in the life of Peter are, however, often parodied, as when in Byron's 'The Vision of Judgment', 'Saint Peter sat by the celestial gate: / His keys were rusty and the lock was dull' (1–2; cf. 121–22, 131–32, 151–52, 197, 825–27); he finds the keys all there is to hand now, since the sword with which he cut off the ear of Malchus has been lost (149–52). John Ruskin is much moved by the final narrative of Jesus' conversation and commissioning of Peter on the beach of Lake Galilee in *Modern Painters* (3.4.16), but imagines in 'Arrows of the Chase' (2.209, 184) that the injunction to 'Feed my sheep' is best understood by a clergyman of refinement most liberally: '... feeding either sheep or fowls, or unmuzzling the ox, or keeping the wrens alive in the snow, would be received by their Heavenly Feeder as the perfect fulfilment of His "Feed my sheep" in the higher sense'. In Tennyson's *Becket* Walter Map tells Herbert of Basham about King Henry's sumptuous banquet: 'And as for the flesh at table, a whole Peter's sheet, with all manner of game, and four footed things, and fowls.' Herbert, recognizing the allusion to Acts 10:9–8, asks, 'And all manner of creeping things too?' In Thackeray's *The Newcomes* the words of Jesus to Peter, 'Thou art Peter, and upon this rock...' (Matthew 16:18), are associated primarily with the Vatican church (chapter 35); and in De Quincey's 'Levana and Our Lady of Sighs,' the eldest sister 'carries keys more than papal at her girdle, which open every cottage and every palace'.

In other cases there is conflation of a biblical passage concerning Peter with a previous literary allusion to it, as when G.B. Shaw, in revising Matthew 16:18, speaks of 'the rock on which Equality is built', or when Wilde seems to recollect Bunyan as well as Matthew 16:18 ('and the gates of hell shall not prevail against it') in his 'The Canterville Ghost', in which the young adventurer is warned: 'You will see fearful shapes in the darkness, and wicked voices will whisper in your ear, but they will not harm you, for against the purity of a little child the powers of hell cannot prevail' (5).

Direct portrayals of Peter, or adaptations from biblical and apocryphal texts, have become more prevalent in the 20th century. Thornton Wilder's play *Now the Servant's Name was Malchus* (1928) and Henry Sienkewicz's novel *Quo Vadis?* (as well as the play based upon it by Marie Doran) were followed by Morris West's novel about the papacy, *The Shoes of the Fisherman*, and Peter Marshall's *The Robe*, in both of which Peter is also given vivid treatment. Peter's irate slicing off of the ear of Malchus is one of the incidents most often alluded to, as in David Jones' *Anathemata* (153). His crucifixion upside down, recalled more rarely, is alluded to in Anthony Hecht's *A Summoning of Stones*:

> ... the Rock that bears the Church's weight,
> Crucified Peter, raised his eyes and yearned
> For final sight of heavenly estate,
> But saw ungainly huge above his head
> Our stony base to which the flesh is wed.
> ('A Roman Holiday')

The two epistles of Peter are frequently referred to, with 1 Peter 4:8 ('For charity shall cover the multitude of sins') being among the most common recollections. Blake repeatedly alludes to this verse in *The Marriage of Heaven and Hell*, and it became a Puritan and Victorian commonplace. Gaskell cites it typically in respect to benevolence in 'The Squire's Story', and in *Walden* Thoreau's benevolent person will exhibit goodness which 'must not be a partial and transitory act, but a constant superfluity, which costs him nothing and of which he is unconscious. This is a charity which hides a multitude of sins' ('Economy'). In another of the familiar passages found in 1 Peter the writer exhorts the other elders to 'Feed the flock of God which is among you, taking the oversight thereof, not by constraint, but willingly; not for filthy lucre, but of a ready mind. Neither as being lords over God's heritage, but being ensamples to the flock' (1 Peter 5:1–3).

Readers of Chaucer's *Canterbury Tales* will recognize that this passage (assisted with commentaries from St Gregory the Great and probably Wyclif) found its way into the description of the good

Parson: 'Benygne he was, and wonder diligent, / and in adversitee ful pacient' (*General Prologue*, 1.483–84; cf. 518); 'This nobel ensaumple to his shepe he yaf, / that first he wroghte, and afterward he taughte' (1.496–97); he demonstrated his belief that 'Wel oghte a preest ensaumple for to yive, / By his clennes, how that his sheep should lyve' (505–06);

> He waited after no pompe and reverence
> Ne maked him a spiced conscience,
> But Cristes lore and his apostles twelve
> He taughte, but first he folwed it hymselve. (525–28)

This way of viewing the relation of person and office in the clergy, urged by Peter (1 Peter 5:3), is in English tradition supported vigorously in exegesis and commentary (e.g., Sedulius Scotus, Aelfric, Fitzralph, Wyclif, Langland, Chaucer) and may in some way account for the relative diminishment of Peter himself in English literature. The good pastor he became, despite his frailty, and which he calls for in this epistle, became a literary type (Langland's Piers, Chaucer's Parson, Herbert's Parson, Fielding's Parson Adams, etc.) and at its best an 'ensaumple' of something greater than Peter himself.

David L. Jeffrey
*University of Ottawa*

## Pontius Pilate

Pontius Pilate ruled from AD26 to 36 as the fifth Roman governor of Judea, Samaria, and Idumaea.

His involvement in the passion of Jesus Christ is recorded in the Gospels (Matthew 27; Mark 15; Luke 23; John 18:29–19:22, 31, 38), the Acts (3:13; 4:27; 13:28), and 1 Timothy (6:13). The evangelists (especially John and Luke) de-emphasize Pilate's responsibility for Christ's death, instead stressing the involvement of the Jews and their leaders. Only Matthew mentions the dream of Pilate's wife and the handwashing scene (Matthew 27:19, 24). Luke writes that Pilate handed Jesus over to Herod, who sent him back (Luke 23:7–12). John reports Pilate's question 'What is truth?' as well as the statements 'Behold the man!' and 'Behold your King!' (John 18:38; 19:5, 14). All four evangelists concur that Pilate originally intended to set Jesus free, but, prompted by the crowd, released Barabbas and had Jesus crucified.

Pilate has been extensively treated as a literary figure both in medieval and modern times. He appears in at least twenty-six European Passion plays, including all of the English cycles. The English often portray him as a braggart, whose pompous rhetoric produces a comical effect. In the Towneley cycle, however, Pilate is consistently depicted as a vicious tyrant. The Towneley 'Play of the Talents' has Pilate gamble, along with Jesus' executioners, for his seamless garment. Although Pilate loses the game, he nevertheless acquires the robe through threats and manipulation. When performed, the role of Pilate was evidently spoken in a 'loud magisterial voice' or a less than magisterial roar – as reflected in Chaucer's 'in Pilates voys he gan to crie' (Miller's Tale, Prologue 1.3124).

The scene in which Pilate, in an act of self-vindication, 'washes his hands' of responsibility for Jesus' fate (see Deuteronomy 21:6–7; cf. Stoephasius, 8, note 4) became a favourite literary motif. (There are also paintings by Duccio, Honthorst, Rembrandt, Turner, and others.) In his Faerie Queene (2.7.61–62) Spenser depicts Pilate as a wretch in Cocytus who washes his hands incessantly, trying in vain to rid himself of his guilt. Shakespeare uses the handwashing motif three times. In Richard 2, 4.1.239–42 the dethroned king condemns his adversaries, equating their sin to that of Pilate. In Richard 3, 1.4.270–71, the Second Murderer expresses his futile desire to wash the guilt from his hands. Likewise in Macbeth, 5.1.26–66, Lady Macbeth is unable to wash Duncan's blood from her hands. Similarly, in a modern context, Arthur Miller's The Crucible (1953) has John Proctor shout at the Reverend Hale: 'Pontius Pilate! God will not let you wash your hands of this!'

Pilate's question about the nature of truth (John 18:38) has been echoed by English writers such as Francis Bacon, William Blake, and Aldous Huxley. Bacon begins his first essay, 'Of Truth', with '"What is Truth?" said jesting Pilate...' – words which become the motto for Huxley's Jesting Pilate: The Diary of a Journey (1928). Blake in his *Annotations to Bacon's Essays* (circa 1798) comments: 'Rational Truth is not the Truth of Christ, but of Pilate. It is the Tree of the Knowledge of Good & Evil' (397). In *The Task* (1785) William Cowper explains: "twas Pilate's question, put / To Truth itself, that deign'd him no reply' (3.270–71). In his unfinished poem 'Pilate' (1862–68) Hopkins presents a Pilate tortured by his conscience, who asks himself what he had asked Christ: 'And what am I?' (118). In the end he seeks redemption by crucifying himself.

Other literary allusions to Pilate are frequent. In *Of Reformation* (47) Milton justifies separation of church and state through Christ's remark to Pilate, 'My kingdom is not of this world' (John 18:36). John Greenleaf Whittier refers to Luke 23:12 (where Pilate and Herod become friends) in his antislavery poem 'Clerical Oppressors' (1836), identifying the pro-slavery Southern clergy with the high priests, who are the allies of the rulers. In his poem 'St Simeon Stylites' (1842) Tennyson links Pilate with Judas Iscariot (165). In Tennyson's play *Becket* (1884) the titular hero opposes the king, exclaiming: 'The Lord be judged again by Pilate? No!' (1.3). George Meredith, in 'The Song of Theodolinda', calls Pilate 'Damned for ever for the deed!' (stanza 11), but G.B. Shaw, in the preface to *Androcles and the Lion* (1916), supports Pilate the politician, who had to consider Jesus a threat to society. In Joseph Conrad's *The Rescue* (1920) 'Pilate appears in the form of the chubby and pious Shaw' (D. Purdy, *Joseph Conrad's Bible*, 1984, 103). James Joyce mentions Pilate in *Ulysses* and irreverently transforms his name to Pontius Pilax in *Finnegans Wake*. In Toni Morrison's novel *The Song of Solomon* (1977) Pilate Dead, whose first name has been randomly chosen from the Bible, is the major female character. In his poem 'What I Have Written I Have Written' (1981) Peter Porter defends his work with Pilate's remark concerning the inscription on the cross (John 19:22).

Pilate is the titular figure in a host of 20th-century English works such as Hilary D.C. Pepler's modern Passion play *Pilate* (1928) and Carlo Maria Franzero's *The Memoirs of Pontius Pilate: From the Autobiography of G. Pontius Pilate* (1947), an amusing account of Pilate's life as a civil servant, written after his governorship in Judea. Paul Luther Maier's *Pontius Pilate: A Biographical Novel* (1968) combines historical facts and rich imagination. Warren Kiefer synthesizes the mystery of archaeology with Jewish persecution in the thriller *The Pontius Pilate Papers* (1976). In the first of his *Rallying Cries: Three Plays* (1977) Eric Bentley draws a parallel between Pilate's examination of Christ and the interrogation of American writers (L. Stander, A. Miller) before the House Committee on Un-American Activities. He compares their refusal to disclose names with Christ's silence (65). The third of these plays, 'From the Memoirs of Pontius Pilate', reveals a Pilate who wants to keep Jesus alive, although Jesus himself has 'decided' to be crucified (179). In *The Pilate Tapes* (1986), a sequence of witty poems, New Zealand's Vincent O'Sullivan places Pilate and the various people associated with him in the modern world.

Pilate provides the title, as well, for a variety of non-English texts, including: *Pilatus* (a German poem of the 12th century with 621 rhymed lines); Anatole France, 'Le procurateur de Judée' (with the surprising conclusion that Pilate is unable to recall Jesus); Luis Coloma, *Pilatillo* (1886); Mario Soldati, *Pilato: Tre atti* (1924); Heinrich Federer, *Pilatus* (1948); Franz Theodor Csokor, 'Pilatus', in his *Olymp und Golgatha* (1954); Werner Koch, *Pilatus: Erinnerungen* (1959; translated *Pontius Pilate Reflects*, 1962); Alexander Lernet-Holenia, *Pilatus: Ein Komplex* (1967); Carlos Heitor Cony, *Pilatos: Romance* (1974); Roger Caillois, *Ponce Pilate: Récit* (1961; translated by Charles Markmann, 1963); Jean Grosjean, *Pilate: Récit* (1983).

Traditionally Pontius Pilate plays a significant role in literature about Jesus Christ. Indeed, in the encounter between Pilate and Christ, the chief representatives of secular and divine power confront each other. The trial, which has been described in literary criticism as a 'discontinuous dialogue', is full of dramatic irony and has served as an endless source of literary inspiration. Sholem Asch, in his play *The Nazarene* (1939), makes Pilate's wife Claudia the daughter of Tiberius Caesar. Pilate thereby becomes the son-in-law of the emperor, the world's ruler, and structurally mirrors Jesus, the Son of God. In his novel *King Jesus* (1946) Robert Graves represents Jesus as the grandson of Herod the Great and Pilate as a pragmatic politician. When Pilate learns that Jesus refuses his claim to the worldly throne and is thus useless to him, he takes a bribe from Herod Antipas and condemns Christ. Anthony Burgess, in his *Man of Nazareth* (1979), depicts Pilate as a mundane man, averse to the priests and weary of his tasks, who ultimately realizes his guilt and shows signs of repentance. In his much-acclaimed Russian novel *The Master and Margarita* (1938) Mikhail Bulgakov stresses Pilate's responsibility for Jesus' death in an original manner and has Herod send Jesus to Pilate, who lets Caiaphas decide between Christ and Barabbas.

Pilate lives on in various place names, often associated with his legendary burial ground. Both Ruskin and Turner produce drawings of a Mount Pilate (*Pilatusberg*) near Lucerne, Switzerland. A nearby lake (*Pilatussee*) was considered to be the haunted final resting place of Pilate. Sir Walter Scott relates the tale of this mountain in *Anne of Geierstein* (chapter 1). A second Mount Pilate is situated in the Rhaetian Alps, a third in the Apennines, and yet another in the Cévennes. (Etymologists contend that these names are corruptions of *pileatus*, meaning 'cloud-capped'.) Pilate is also thought to be buried in Vienne, in the Rhone valley.

Critical and literary representations of Pontius Pilate comprise the whole gamut of characterizations: he has been depicted as a sly and effective politician, a ruthless but reliable soldier, a sceptic and a cynic, an able yet corrupt administrator, a well-meaning but vacillating judge, both the adversary and an instrument of God, a devil and a saint – or simply an imperfect man. For Christians who profess the Creed, however, it matters only that Jesus Christ 'suffered under Pontius Pilate'.

Peter Groth
*Universität Hamburg, Germany*

## Thomas, Doubting

St Thomas, who was not present at Jesus' first post-resurrection appearance to his gathered disciples, was incredulous at the claims of the others to have seen the risen Christ and protested, 'Except I shall see in his hands the print of the nails, and put my finger into the print of the nails, and thrust my hand into his side, I will not believe' (John 20:19–25). Eight days later, as the disciples were assembled once again, Jesus suddenly 'stood in their midst' and addressed Thomas: 'Reach hither thy finger, and behold my hands; and reach hither thy hand, and thrust it into my side, and be not faithless, but believing' (20:26–27). Appalled and ashamed, Thomas uttered his acknowledgment: 'My Lord and my God', to which Jesus replied, 'Thomas, because thou hast seen me, thou hast believed: blessed are they that have not seen, and yet have believed' (20:28–29).

The Aramaic form of Thomas' Greek name means 'the twin', and the Greek name, 'Didymus' ('twin'), is attached to him in several places (John 11:16; 20:24; 21:2). In Syriac and gnostic tradition Thomas is called Judas Thomas and identified with the 'Judas (not Iscariot)' of John 14:22. He figures only in the fourth Gospel, though an apocryphal Gospel of Thomas (2nd century) concerning the infancy of Jesus and a late 2nd- or early 3rd-century Acts of St Thomas (subsequently elaborated) describe his being sent to India as a missionary by the other apostles in Jerusalem. When he resisted, these legends relate, he was sold as a slave to the messenger of the Indian king and arrived thus at his destination (much in the manner of the reluctant prophet Jonah).

'Doubting Thomas' is remembered in incidental reference in a variety of English texts, such as H.G. Wells' *The Undying Fire*, in which the sceptical Dr Barrack proclaims, 'I want things I can feel and handle. I am an Agnostic by nature and habit and profession. A *Doubting Thomas*, born and bred.' More substantial allusions are rare, and Thomas himself has a minimal role except in dramatic reenactments of the Passion and resurrection, where his confession of faith, as well as his initial doubt, is recalled. In her play cycle *The Man Born to Be King* (1943), Dorothy L. Sayers calls attention to the signal irony that 'the one absolutely unequivocal statement, in the whole Gospel, of the Divinity of Jesus... come[s] from Doubting Thomas. It is the only place where the word 'God' is used of him without qualification of any kind, and in the most unambiguous form of words (not merely *theos* but *ho theos mou* with the definite article).'

David L. Jeffrey
*University of Ottawa*

85

## Woman of Samaria

The story of Jesus' encounter with the Samaritan woman at the well
and his offering her a 'well of water springing up into everlasting life'
(John 4:4–42) is one of the more complex narratives in the ministry
sections of the Gospels. It involves cultural conflict (Samaritans vs.
Jews), sex role issues (a woman married five times who meets and
recognizes Jesus), an episode in the education of the disciples, and
highly symbolic language ('water of life' and the end of 'spiritual
thirst'). The story bears a typological relationship with several Genesis
narratives and constitutes one of the famous dialogues in John's
Gospel (e.g., 3:1–5, Nicodemus; 6:25–59; 8:12–59, crowds;
11:17–44, Martha and Mary). Narratively, the story functions to show
Jesus as the promised Messiah, who fulfils Jewish hopes of
redemption and who also comes to bring redemption to all peoples.

The setting of the conversation is reminiscent of betrothal stories
which occur at wells – stories of Rebecca (Genesis 24:10–14), Rachel
(Genesis 29:1–12), and the daughters of the priest of Midian (Exodus
2:15–21). 'Living waters' (a wordplay on a Semitic expression for
flowing water) has a rich Old Testament background as a symbol for
divine, life-giving activity (e.g., Jeremiah 2:13; Ezekiel 47:9; Zechariah
14:8). Water is such a symbol elsewhere in John also (e.g., 7:37;
19:34). In medieval and Renaissance exegetical writing the typology of
the waters of life is linked to the fountain of Eden (Genesis 2:10–14),
the crossing of the Red Sea (Exodus 14:21–29), the rock of Horeb
(Exodus 17:6), and the sealed fountain (Song of Solomon 4:12). In
sacramental terms it is associated with the grace of the baptismal waters
and, in conjunction with the rock of Horeb, it is also associated with the
blood which flowed from Christ's side. In eschatological terms it
prefigures the pure river of water (Revelation 22:1).

Extracanonical legends give the Samaritan woman the name
St Photine and record that she preached the gospel, was imprisoned for
three years, and died for her faith in Carthage. In another apocryphal
narrative she is said to have been martyred in Rome after converting the
daughter of Nero and 100 of her retinue. Her feast day is March 20.

Perhaps the best-known use of the story in medieval literature
is the reference made to the Samaritan woman by the Wife of Bath in

the prologue to her tale. She justifies her own robust sexuality by boasting that she, too, has had five husbands. She claims not to know what Jesus meant by the remark that the 'sixth man' she has now is not her husband. D.W. Robertson has argued that the Samaritan woman, who achieves sublime wisdom, provides an ironic contrast with the Wife, who cannot understand Christ's words and is therefore a 'literary personification of rampant "femininity" or carnality, and her exegesis is, in consequence, rigorously carnal and literal' (*A Preface to Chaucer*, 1962, 318–22). She pretentiously challenges Christ's teaching of the spirit, favouring the Old Law, where 'God bad us for to wexe and multiplye; / That gentil text kan I wel understonde' (Chaucer, *Canterbury Tales*, 3.28–29).

The typological reading of the well in Samaria as the well of life and a symbol of baptism and regeneration was popular through the 16th and 17th centuries. Edmund Spenser uses the well of life with its rejuvenative connotations in *The Faerie Queene* (1.2.43 and 1.11.29). Among the metaphysical poets, Herbert, Vaughan, and Traherne employed the imagery of redeeming waters. Vaughan makes explicit reference to the Samaritan woman's visit to Jacob's Well in 'The Search', but unlike her he does not find his answers in experience. In 'Religion', in which Vaughan employs the typology of the closed fountain of Song of Solomon 4:12, he describes religion as a 'tainted sink... like that Samaritans dead well' (*Silex Scintillans*).

Edward Taylor's meditations bring together his desire for spiritual awareness with his preparations for the Lord's Supper. He joins the Samaritan's experience at the well with the typology from Genesis, 'the Well of Living Water and Tree of Life', to which he adds the sacramental dimension, 'Lord bath mee in this Well of Life' (*Preparatory Meditations*, 2.47). Christopher Smart includes the story in his verse paraphrases, *The Parables of Our Lord and Saviour Jesus Christ* (1768). He adheres closely to the biblical account, emphasizing Christ's knowledge of the woman's marital history and her astonishment at his prophetic vision. He draws no conclusions about her past life, the immorality of successive marriages, and the problem of her current status but rather uses the episode to reveal Christ's marvellous omniscience. In Emily Dickinson's 'I know where Wells grow –' the poet grapples with the idea of spiritual thirst: 'I read in an Old fashioned Book / That People "thirst no more" –' But she finds that her thirst is better satisfied by 'a little Well – like Mine – / Dearer to understand'.

Edmond Rostand's biblical drama *The Woman of Samaria*, first performed in 1897, reflects on the ancient significance of the well and the Jewish–Samaritan conflict as it opens with the phantoms of Abraham, Isaac, and Jacob. The revolutionary rhetoric of a young Samaritan sustains the political concerns of the story. Photine, Rostand's heroine, approaches Christ at the well, singing songs of love from the Song of Solomon. These songs continue through the play, though they gain symbolic meaning as her own awareness deepens from carnal to spiritual knowledge. Rostand makes little of Photine's moral history, though he does add the character of Azriel, Photine's sixth man, who is astonished when this illiterate woman learns to expound Scripture like an ecstatic preacher. The play includes pageantry and Photine's exuberant singing. Even the otherwise crusty disciples eventually join in the celebration of love.

Faye Pauli Whitaker
*Iowa State University*

## Woman Taken in Adultery

When the scribes and Pharisees wished to entrap Jesus concerning his regard for the Mosaic law, they apprehended a woman in the act of adultery and brought her to him, saying,

> Now Moses in the law commanded us, that such should be stoned: but what sayest thou? This they said, tempting him, that they might have [something with which] to accuse him. But Jesus stooped down, and with his finger wrote on the ground, as though he heard them not. So when they continued asking him, he lifted up himself, and said unto them, He that is without sin among you, let him [be the] first [to] cast a stone at her. And again he stooped down, and wrote on the ground. (John 8:5–8)

At this the accusers of the woman withdrew, one by one, until Jesus was left alone with her. He then asked her, 'Woman, where are those thine accusers? hath no man condemned thee? She said, No man,

Lord. And Jesus said unto her, Neither do I condemn thee: go, and sin no more' (8:9–12).

When Chaucer has Alisoun of *The Miller's Tale* put off Absolon the amorous deacon while she commits adultery with Nicholas the student, he gives her the words 'Go forth thy wey, or I wol caste a ston' (1.3712), a transparent and crude reversal of Christ's words to the adulterous woman which underscores Alisoun's wilful culpability. Chaucer's Parson in his sermon is unstinting in his condemnation of 'Avowtrie', which he says is set between theft and homicide in the Decalogue, 'for it is the gretteste theft that may be, for it is thefte of body and of soule. / And it is lyk to homycide, for it kerveth atwo and breketh atwo hem that first were maked o flessh. And therfore, by the olde lawe of God, they sholde be slayn.' But, he adds,

> natheless, by the lawe of Jhesu Crist, that is lawe of pitee, when he seyde to the womman that was founden in avowtrie, and sholde han been slayn with stones... 'Go', quod Jhesu Crist, 'and have namoore wyl to do synne.'... Soothly the vengeaunce of Avowtrie is awarded to the peynes of helle, but if so be that it be destourbed [prevented] by penitence. (886–90)

In Shakespeare's *Measure for Measure*, a man is 'taken in adultery' – actually fornication – and by the Puritan 'protector' Angelo condemned to death despite his sister's pleas for mercy, so as not to 'make a scarecrow of the law' (2.1.1). In Angelo's words (2.1.27–31):

> You may not so extenuate his offence
> For I have had such faults; but rather tell me,
> When I, that censure him, do so offend,
> Let mine own judgment pattern out my death,
> And nothing come in partial. Sir, he must die.

When Isabella's pleas for mercy for her brother result only in Angelo's lustful proposition that she trade her honour for her brother's life, and that villainy in turn is, with other breaches, uncovered, the accuser here too is robbed of his appeal to justice and must depend upon mercy. Because 'grace is grace, despite of all controversy' (1.2.25–27), he too then receives mercy when the lesson is learned and repentance ensues.

In literature since the 18th century there has been a tendency to apply the text as an appeal for toleration as much as for mercy. In his preface to *Adonaïs* Shelley compares the accusers in the narrative to the critics he feels have hastened Keats to an early grave: 'Against what woman taken in adultery dares the foremost of these literary prostitutes to cast his opprobrious stone? Miserable man! You, one of the meanest, have wantonly defaced one of the noblest specimens of the workmanship of God.' William Morris, in *News from Nowhere*, takes this application one step further, claiming that in Utopia legal penalties are bound to be mild: 'Paying a severe legal penalty, the wrongdoer can "go and sin again" with comfort... Remember Jesus had got the legal penalty remitted before he said "Go and sin no more."' When Miss Prism's erstwhile maternity (hence adultery) is revealed to her in the third act of Oscar Wilde's *The Importance of Being Earnest*, she recoils 'in indignant astonishment': 'Mr Worthing! I am unmarried!' to which Jack replies, 'Unmarried! I do not deny that is a serious blow. But after all, who has the right to cast a stone against the one who has suffered? Cannot repentance wipe out the act of folly? Why should there be one law for men, and another for women?'

David L. Jeffrey
*University of Ottawa*

# THE GOSPEL OF ST JOHN

Prologue – The Light of the World     *93*

## Part One: The Light Revealed

The Witness of John the Baptist     *95*

Jesus Calls the First Disciples     *96*

The First Sign: The Wedding at Cana     *97*

The Cleansing of the Temple     *97*

'You Must be Born from Above'     *98*

John Bears Witness Again     *100*

The Woman of Samaria     *101*

The Second Sign: Jesus Heals a Royal Official's Son     *104*

The Third Sign: Jesus Heals a Man at the Pool of Bethesda     *104*

The Fourth Sign: The Feeding of the Five Thousand     *108*

Jesus Walks on the Water     *108*

The Bread of Life     *109*

Jesus Teaches in the Temple     *112*

The Woman Taken in Adultery     *115*

'The Truth Will Set you Free'     *116*

The Fifth Sign: Jesus Heals a Man Born Blind     *121*

The Good Shepherd     *123*

The Sixth Sign: The Raising of Lazarus     *126*

## Part Two: The Darkness Defeated

Mary Anoints Jesus    130

Jesus Enters Jerusalem    130

Jesus Washes his Disciples' Feet    134

'Love One Another'    135

The Way, the Truth and the Life    136

The True Vine    139

'I Have Conquered the World'    141

Jesus Prays for his Disciples    145

Judas Betrays his Master    147

Peter's Denial    148

The Trial Before Pilate    149

The Crucifixion    150

The Entombment    151

The Resurrection    152

Epilogue – The Seventh Sign:
Jesus' Last Appearance to his Disciples    154

# PROLOGUE – THE LIGHT OF THE WORLD
John 1:1–18

In the beginning was the Word:
the Word was with God
and the Word was God.
He was with God in the beginning.
Through him all things came into being,
not one thing came into being except through him.
What has come into being in him was life,
life that was the light of men;
and light shines in darkness,
and darkness could not overpower it.

A man came, sent by God.
His name was John.
He came as a witness, to bear witness to the light,
so that everyone might believe through him.
He was not the light,
he was to bear witness to the light.

The Word was the real light
that gives light to everyone;
he was coming into the world.
He was in the world
that had come into being through him,
and the world did not recognize him.
He came to his own
and his own people did not accept him.
But to those who did accept him
he gave power to become children of God,
to those who believed in his name
who were born not from human stock
or human desire
or human will
but from God himself.

The Word became flesh,
he lived among us,
and we saw his glory,
the glory that he has from the Father as only Son of
    the Father,
full of grace and truth.

John witnesses to him. He proclaims:
'This is the one of whom I said:
He who comes after me
has passed ahead of me
because he existed before me.'

Indeed, from his fullness we have, all of us, received –
one gift replacing another,
for the Law was given through Moses,
grace and truth have come through Jesus Christ.
No one has ever seen God;
it is the only Son, who is close to the Father's heart,
who has made him known.

## Part One

# The Light Revealed

### THE WITNESS OF JOHN THE BAPTIST
John 1:19–34

This was the witness of John, when the Jews sent to him priests and Levites from Jerusalem to ask him, 'Who are you?' He declared, he did not deny but declared, 'I am not the Christ.' So they asked, 'Then are you Elijah?' He replied, 'I am not.' 'Are you the Prophet?' He answered, 'No.' So they said to him, 'Who are you? We must take back an answer to those who sent us. What have you to say about yourself?' So he said, 'I am, as Isaiah prophesied:

A voice of one that cries in the desert:
'Prepare a way for the Lord.
Make his paths straight!'

Now those who had been sent were Pharisees, and they put this question to him, 'Why are you baptizing if you are not the Christ, and not Elijah, and not the Prophet?' John answered them, 'I baptise with water; but standing among you – unknown to you – is the one who is coming after me; and I am not fit to undo the strap of his sandal.' This happened at Bethany, on the far side of the Jordan, where John was baptizing.

The next day, he saw Jesus coming towards him and said, 'Look, there is the lamb of God that takes away the sin of the world. It was of him that I said, "Behind me comes one who has passed ahead of me because he existed before me." I did not know him myself, and yet my purpose in coming to baptize with water was so that he might be revealed to Israel.' And John declared, 'I saw the Spirit come down on him like a dove from heaven and rest on him. I did not know him myself, but he who sent me to baptize with water had said to me, "The man on whom you see the Spirit come down and rest is the one who is to baptize with the Holy Spirit." I have seen and I testify that he is the Chosen One of God.'

## JESUS CALLS THE FIRST DISCIPLES
### John 1:35–51

The next day as John stood there again with two of his disciples, Jesus went past, and John looked towards him and said, 'Look, there is the lamb of God.' And the two disciples heard what he said and followed Jesus. Jesus turned round, saw them following and said, 'What do you want?' They answered, 'Rabbi' – which means Teacher – 'where do you live?' He replied, 'Come and see'; so they went and saw where he lived, and stayed with him that day. It was about the tenth hour.

One of these two who became followers of Jesus after hearing what John had said was Andrew, the brother of Simon Peter. The first thing Andrew did was to find his brother and say to him, 'We have found the Messiah' – which means the Christ – and he took Simon to Jesus. Jesus looked at him and said, 'You are Simon son of John; you are to be called Cephas' – which means Rock.

The next day, after Jesus had decided to leave for Galilee, he met Philip and said, 'Follow me.' Philip came from the same town, Bethsaida, as Andrew and Peter.

Philip found Nathanael and said to him, 'We have found him of whom Moses in the Law and the prophets wrote, Jesus son of Joseph, from Nazareth.' Nathanael said to him, 'From Nazareth? Can anything good come from that place?' Philip replied, 'Come and see.' When Jesus saw Nathanael coming he said of him, 'There, truly, is an Israelite in whom there is no deception.' Nathanael asked, 'How do you know me?' Jesus replied, 'Before Philip came to call you, I saw you under the fig tree.' Nathanael answered, 'Rabbi, you are the Son of God, you are the king of Israel.' Jesus replied, 'You believe that just because I said: I saw you under the fig tree. You are going to see greater things than that.' And then he added, 'In all truth I tell you, you will see heaven open and the angels of God ascending and descending over the Son of man.'

## THE FIRST SIGN: THE WEDDING AT CANA
John 2:1-11

On the third day there was a wedding at Cana in Galilee. The mother of Jesus was there, and Jesus and his disciples had also been invited. And they ran out of wine, since the wine provided for the feast had all been used, and the mother of Jesus said to him, 'They have no wine.' Jesus said, 'Woman, what do you want from me? My hour has not come yet.' His mother said to the servants, 'Do whatever he tells you.' There were six stone water jars standing there, meant for the ablutions that are customary among the Jews: each could hold twenty or thirty gallons. Jesus said to the servants, 'Fill the jars with water,' and they filled them to the brim. Then he said to them, 'Draw some out now and take it to the president of the feast.' They did this; the president tasted the water, and it had turned into wine. Having no idea where it came from – though the servants who had drawn the water knew – the president of the feast called the bridegroom and said, 'Everyone serves good wine first and the worse wine when the guests are well wined; but you have kept the best wine till now.'

This was the first of Jesus' signs: it was at Cana in Galilee. He revealed his glory, and his disciples believed in him.

## THE CLEANSING OF THE TEMPLE
John 2:12-25

After this he went down to Capernaum with his mother and his brothers and his disciples, but they stayed there only a few days.

When the time of the Jewish Passover was near Jesus went up to Jerusalem, and in the Temple he found people selling cattle and sheep and doves, and the money changers sitting there. Making a whip out of cord, he drove them all out of the Temple, sheep and cattle as well, scattered the money changers' coins, knocked their tables over and said to the dove sellers, 'Take all this out of here and stop using my Father's house as a market.' Then his disciples remembered the words of scripture: 'I am eaten up with zeal for your house.' The Jews intervened and said, 'What sign can you show us that you should act like this?' Jesus answered, 'Destroy this Temple, and in three days I will raise it up.' The Jews replied, 'It has taken forty-six years to build this Temple: are you going to raise it up again in three days?' But he was speaking of the Temple that was his body, and when Jesus rose from the dead, his disciples remembered that he had said this, and they believed the scripture and what he had said.

During his stay in Jerusalem for the feast of the Passover many believed in his name when they saw the signs that he did, but Jesus knew all people and did not trust himself to them; he never needed evidence about anyone; he could tell what someone had within.

## 'YOU MUST BE BORN FROM ABOVE'
### John 3:1–21

There was one of the Pharisees called Nicodemus, a leader of the Jews, who came to Jesus by night and said, 'Rabbi, we know that you have come from God as a teacher; for no one could perform the signs that you do unless God were with him.' Jesus answered:

> In all truth I tell you,
> no one can see the kingdom of God
> without being born from above.

Nicodemus said, 'How can anyone who is already old be born? Is it possible to go back into the womb again and be born?' Jesus replied:

> In all truth I tell you,
> no one can enter the kingdom of God
> without being born through water and the Spirit;
> what is born of human nature is human;
> what is born of the Spirit is spirit.
> Do not be surprised when I say:
> You must be born from above.
> The wind blows where it pleases;
> you can hear its sound,
> but you cannot tell where it comes from or where it is going.
> So it is with everyone who is born of the Spirit.

'How is that possible?' asked Nicodemus. Jesus replied, 'You are the Teacher of Israel, and you do not know these things!

In all truth I tell you,
we speak only about what we know
and witness only to what we have seen
and yet you people reject our evidence.
If you do not believe me
when I speak to you about earthly things,
how will you believe me
when I speak to you about heavenly things?
No one has gone up to heaven
except the one who came down from heaven,
the Son of man;
as Moses lifted up the snake in the desert,
so must the Son of man be lifted up
so that everyone who believes may have eternal life in him.
For this is how God loved the world:
he gave his only Son,
so that everyone who believes in him may not perish
but may have eternal life.
For God sent his Son into the world
not to judge the world,
but so that through him the world might be saved.
No one who believes in him will be judged;
but whoever does not believe is judged already,
because that person does not believe
in the Name of God's only Son.
And the judgment is this:
though the light has come into the world
people have preferred
darkness to the light
because their deeds were evil.
And indeed, everybody who does wrong
hates the light and avoids it,
to prevent his actions from being shown up;
but whoever does the truth

comes out into the light,
so that what he is doing may plainly appear as done in God.

## JOHN BEARS WITNESS AGAIN
John 3:22–36

After this, Jesus went with his disciples into the Judean countryside
and stayed with them there and baptized. John also was baptizing at
Aenon near Salim, where there was plenty of water, and people were
going there and were being baptized. For John had not yet been put
in prison.

Now a discussion arose between some of John's disciples and a
Jew about purification, so they went to John and said, 'Rabbi, the man
who was with you on the far side of the Jordan, the man to whom you
bore witness, is baptizing now, and everyone is going to him.' John
replied:

No one can have anything
except what is given him from heaven.

'You yourselves can bear me out. I said, "I am not the Christ; I am the
one who has been sent to go in front of him."'

It is the bridegroom who has the bride;
and yet the bridegroom's friend,
who stands there and listens to him,
is filled with joy at the bridegroom's voice.
This is the joy I feel, and it is complete.
He must grow greater,
I must grow less.
He who comes from above
is above all others;
he who is of the earth
is earthly himself and speaks in an earthly way.
He who comes from heaven
bears witness to the things he has seen and heard,

but his testimony is not accepted by anybody;
though anyone who does accept his testimony
is attesting that God is true,
since he whom God has sent
speaks God's own words,
for God gives him the Spirit without reserve.
The Father loves the Son
and has entrusted everything to his hands.
Anyone who believes in the Son has eternal life,
but anyone who refuses to believe in the Son will never see life:
God's retribution hangs over him.

# THE WOMAN OF SAMARIA
## John 4:1–42

When Jesus heard that the Pharisees had found out that he was
making and baptizing more disciples than John – though in fact it was
his disciples who baptized, not Jesus himself – he left Judea and went
back to Galilee. He had to pass through Samaria. On the way he came
to the Samaritan town called Sychar near the land that Jacob gave to
his son Joseph. Jacob's well was there and Jesus, tired by the journey,
sat down by the well. It was about the sixth hour. When a Samaritan
woman came to draw water, Jesus said to her, 'Give me something to
drink.' His disciples had gone into the town to buy food. The
Samaritan woman said to him, 'You are a Jew. How is it that you ask
me, a Samaritan, for something to drink?' – Jews, of course, do not
associate with Samaritans. Jesus replied to her:

If you only knew what God is offering
and who it is that is saying to you,
'Give me something to drink,'
you would have been the one to ask,
and he would have given you living water.

'You have no bucket, sir,' she answered, 'and the well is deep: how do
you get this living water? Are you a greater man than our father Jacob,

who gave us this well and drank from it himself with his sons and his cattle?' Jesus replied:

> Whoever drinks this water
> will be thirsty again;
> but no one who drinks the water that I shall give
> will ever be thirsty again:
> the water that I shall give
> will become a spring of water within, welling up for eternal life.

'Sir,' said the woman, 'give me some of that water, so that I may never be thirsty or come here again to draw water.' 'Go and call your husband,' said Jesus to her, 'and come back here.' The woman answered, 'I have no husband.' Jesus said to her, 'You are right to say, "I have no husband"; for although you have had five, the one you now have is not your husband. You spoke the truth there.' 'I see you are a prophet, sir,' said the woman. 'Our fathers worshipped on this mountain, though you say that Jerusalem is the place where one ought to worship.' Jesus said:

> Believe me, woman, the hour is coming
> when you will worship the Father
> neither on this mountain nor in Jerusalem.
> You worship what you do not know;
> we worship what we do know;
> for salvation comes from the Jews.
> But the hour is coming – indeed is already here –
> when true worshippers will worship the Father in spirit
>     and truth:
> that is the kind of worshipper
> the Father seeks.
> God is spirit,
> and those who worship
> must worship in spirit and truth.

The woman said to him, 'I know that Messiah – that is, Christ – is coming; and when he comes he will explain everything.' Jesus said, 'That is who I am, I who speak to you.'

At this point his disciples returned and were surprised to find him speaking to a woman, though none of them asked, 'What do you want from her?' or, 'What are you talking to her about?' The woman put down her water jar and hurried back to the town to tell the people, 'Come and see a man who has told me everything I have done; could this be the Christ?' This brought people out of the town and they made their way towards him.

Meanwhile, the disciples were urging him, 'Rabbi, do have something to eat'; but he said, 'I have food to eat that you do not know about.' So the disciples said to one another, 'Has someone brought him food?' But Jesus said:

> My food
> is to do the will of the one who sent me,
> and to complete his work.
> Do you not have a saying:
> Four months and then the harvest?
> Well, I tell you,
> look around you, look at the fields;
> already they are white, ready for harvest!
> Already the reaper is being paid his wages,
> already he is bringing in the grain for eternal life,
> so that sower and reaper can rejoice together.
> For here the proverb holds true:
> one sows, another reaps;
> I sent you to reap
> a harvest you have not laboured for.
> Others have laboured for it;
> and you have come into the rewards of their labour.

Many Samaritans of that town believed in him on the strength of the woman's words of testimony, 'He told me everything I have done.' So, when the Samaritans came up to him, they begged him to stay with them. He stayed for two days, and many more came to believe on the strength of the words he spoke to them; and they said to the woman, 'Now we believe no longer because of what you told us; we have heard him ourselves and we know that he is indeed the Saviour of the world.'

## THE SECOND SIGN: JESUS HEALS
## A ROYAL OFFICIAL'S SON
### John 4:43–54

When the two days were over Jesus left for Galilee. He himself had declared that a prophet is not honoured in his own home town. On his arrival the Galileans received him well, having seen all that he had done at Jerusalem during the festival which they too had attended.

He went again to Cana in Galilee, where he had changed the water into wine. And there was a royal official whose son was ill at Capernaum; hearing that Jesus had arrived in Galilee from Judea, he went and asked him to come and cure his son, as he was at the point of death. Jesus said to him, 'Unless you see signs and portents you will not believe!' 'Sir,' answered the official, 'come down before my child dies.' 'Go home,' said Jesus, 'your son will live.' The man believed what Jesus had said and went on his way home; and while he was still on the way his servants met him with the news that his boy was alive. He asked them when the boy had begun to recover. They replied, 'The fever left him yesterday at the seventh hour.' The father realized that this was exactly the time when Jesus had said, 'Your son will live'; and he and all his household believed.

This new sign, the second, Jesus performed on his return from Judea to Galilee.

## THE THIRD SIGN: JESUS HEALS
## A MAN AT THE POOL OF BETHESDA
### John 5

After this there was a Jewish festival, and Jesus went up to Jerusalem. Now in Jerusalem next to the Sheep Pool there is a pool called Bethesda in Hebrew, which has five porticos; and under these were crowds of sick people, blind, lame, paralysed [waiting for the water to move; for at intervals the angel of the Lord came down into the pool, and the water was disturbed, and the first person to enter the water after this disturbance was cured of any ailment from which he was suffering.] One man there had an illness which had lasted thirty-eight years, and when Jesus saw him lying there and knew he had been in that condition for a long time, he said, 'Do you want to be well again?' 'Sir,' replied the sick man. 'I have no one to put me into the pool when the water is disturbed; and while I am still on the way, someone else gets down there before me.' Jesus said, 'Get up, pick up your sleeping-mat and walk around.' The man was cured at once, and he picked up his mat and started to walk around.

Now that day happened to be the Sabbath, so the Jews said to the man who had been cured, 'It is the Sabbath; you are not allowed to carry your sleeping-mat.' He replied, 'But the man who cured me told me, "Pick up your sleeping-mat and walk around."' They asked, 'Who is the man who said to you, "Pick up your sleeping-mat and walk around"?' The man had no idea who it was, since Jesus had disappeared, as the place was crowded. After a while Jesus met him in the Temple and said, 'Now you are well again, do not sin any more, or something worse may happen to you.' The man went back and told the Jews that it was Jesus who had cured him. It was because he did things like this on the Sabbath that the Jews began to harass Jesus. His answer to them was, 'My Father still goes on working, and I am at work, too.' But that only made the Jews even more intent on killing him, because not only was he breaking the Sabbath, but he spoke of God as his own Father and so made himself God's equal.

To this Jesus replied:

In all truth I tell you,
by himself the Son can do nothing;
he can do only what he sees the Father doing:
and whatever the Father does the Son does too.
For the Father loves the Son
and shows him everything he himself does,
and he will show him even greater things than these,
works that will astonish you.
Thus, as the Father raises the dead and gives them life,
so the Son gives life to anyone he chooses;
for the Father judges no one;
he has entrusted all judgment to the Son,
so that all may honour the Son

as they honour the Father.
Whoever refuses honour to the Son
refuses honour to the Father who sent him.
In all truth I tell you,
whoever listens to my words,
and believes in the one who sent me,
has eternal life;
without being brought to judgment
such a person has passed from death to life.
In all truth I tell you,
the hour is coming – indeed it is already here –
when the dead will hear the voice of the Son of God,
and all who hear it will live.
For as the Father has life in himself,
so he has granted the Son also to have life in himself;
and, because he is the Son of man,
has granted him power to give judgment.
Do not be surprised at this,
for the hour is coming
when the dead will leave their graves
at the sound of his voice:
those who did good
will come forth to life;
and those who did evil will come forth to judgment.
By myself I can do nothing;
I can judge only as I am told to judge,
and my judging is just,
because I seek to do not my own will
but the will of him who sent me.
Were I to testify on my own behalf,
my testimony would not be true;
but there is another witness who speaks on my behalf,
and I know that his testimony is true.
You sent messengers to John,
and he gave his testimony to the truth –
not that I depend on human testimony;
no, it is for your salvation that I mention it.

John was a lamp lit and shining
and for a time you were content to enjoy the light that he gave.
But my testimony is greater than John's:
the deeds my Father has given me to perform,
these same deeds of mine
testify that the Father has sent me.
Besides, the Father who sent me
bears witness to me himself.
You have never heard his voice,
you have never seen his shape,
and his word finds no home in you
because you do not believe
in the one whom he has sent.

You pore over the scriptures,
believing that in them you can find eternal life;
it is these scriptures that testify to me,
and yet you refuse to come to me to receive life!
Human glory means nothing to me.
Besides, I know you too well:
you have no love of God in you.
I have come in the name of my Father
and you refuse to accept me;
if someone else should come in his own name
you would accept him.
How can you believe,
since you look to each other for glory
and are not concerned
with the glory that comes from the one God?
Do not imagine that I am going to accuse you before the Father:
you have placed your hopes on Moses,
and Moses will be the one who accuses you.
If you really believed him
you would believe me too,
since it was about me that he was writing;
but if you will not believe what he wrote,
how can you believe what I say?

# THE FOURTH SIGN:
# THE FEEDING OF THE FIVE THOUSAND
John 6:1–15

After this, Jesus crossed the Sea of Galilee – or of Tiberias – and a large crowd followed him, impressed by the signs he had done in curing the sick. Jesus climbed the hillside and sat down there with his disciples. The time of the Jewish Passover was near.

Looking up, Jesus saw the crowds approaching and said to Philip, 'Where can we buy some bread for these people to eat?' He said this only to put Philip to the test; he himself knew exactly what he was going to do. Philip answered, 'Two hundred denarii would not buy enough to give them a little piece each.' One of his disciples, Andrew, Simon Peter's brother, said, 'Here is a small boy with five barley loaves and two fish; but what is that among so many?' Jesus said to them, 'Make the people sit down.' There was plenty of grass there, and as many as five thousand men sat down. Then Jesus took the loaves, gave thanks, and distributed them to those who were sitting there; he then did the same with the fish, distributing as much as they wanted. When they had eaten enough he said to the disciples, 'Pick up the pieces left over, so that nothing is wasted.' So they picked them up and filled twelve large baskets with scraps left over from the meal of five barley loaves. Seeing the sign that he had done, the people said, 'This is indeed the prophet who is to come into the world.' Jesus, as he realized they were about to come and take him by force and make him king, fled back to the hills alone.

# JESUS WALKS ON THE WATER
John 6:16–21

That evening the disciples went down to the shore of the sea and got into a boat to make for Capernaum on the other side of the sea. It was getting dark by now and Jesus had still not rejoined them. The wind was strong, and the sea was getting rough. They had rowed three or four miles when they saw Jesus walking on the sea and coming towards the boat. They were afraid, but he said, 'It's me. Don't be afraid.' They were ready to take him into the boat, and immediately it reached the shore at the place they were making for.

## THE BREAD OF LIFE
John 6:22–71

Next day, the crowd that had stayed on the other side saw that only one boat had been there, and that Jesus had not got into the boat with his disciples, but that the disciples had set off by themselves. Other boats, however, had put in from Tiberias, near the place where the bread had been eaten. When the people saw that neither Jesus nor his disciples were there, they got into those boats and crossed to Capernaum to look for Jesus. When they found him on the other side, they said to him, 'Rabbi, when did you come here?' Jesus answered:

> In all truth I tell you,
> you are looking for me
> not because you have seen the signs
> but because you had all the bread you wanted to eat.
> Do not work for food that goes bad,
> but work for food that endures for eternal life,
> which the Son of man will give you,
> for on him the Father, God himself, has set his seal.

Then they said to him, 'What must we do if we are to carry out God's work?' Jesus gave them this answer, 'This is carrying out God's work: you must believe in the one he has sent.' So they said, 'What sign will you yourself do, the sight of which will make us believe in you? What work will you do? Our fathers ate manna in the desert; as scripture says: "He gave them bread from heaven to eat."'

Jesus answered them:

> In all truth I tell you,
> it was not Moses who gave you the bread from heaven,
> it is my Father who gives you the bread from heaven,
> the true bread;
> for the bread of God

is the bread which comes down from heaven
and gives life to the world.

'Sir,' they said, 'give us that bread always.' Jesus answered them:

I am the bread of life.
No one who comes to me will ever hunger;
no one who believes in me will ever thirst.
But, as I have told you,
you can see me and still you do not believe.
Everyone whom the Father gives me will come to me;
I will certainly not reject anyone who comes to me,
because I have come from heaven,
not to do my own will,
but to do the will of him who sent me.
Now the will of him who sent me
is that I should lose nothing
of all that he has given to me,
but that I should raise it up on the last day.
It is my Father's will
that whoever sees the Son and believes in him
should have eternal life,
and that I should raise that person up on the last day.

Meanwhile the Jews were complaining to each other about him, because he had said, 'I am the bread that has come down from heaven.' They were saying, 'Surely this is Jesus son of Joseph, whose father and mother we know. How can he now say, "I have come down from heaven?"' Jesus said in reply to them, 'Stop complaining to each other.'

No one can come to me
unless drawn by the Father who sent me,
and I will raise that person up on the last day.
It is written in the prophets:
'They will all be taught by God';
everyone who has listened to the Father,
and learnt from him,
comes to me.

Not that anybody has seen the Father,
except him who has his being from God:
he has seen the Father.
In all truth I tell you,
everyone who believes has eternal life.
I am the bread of life.
Your fathers ate manna in the desert
and they are dead;
but this is the bread which comes down from heaven,
so that a person may eat it and not die.
I am the living bread which has come down from heaven.
Anyone who eats this bread will live for ever;
and the bread that I shall give
is my flesh, for the life of the world.

Then the Jews started arguing among themselves, 'How can this man give us his flesh to eat?' Jesus replied to them:

In all truth I tell you,
if you do not eat the flesh of the Son of man
and drink his blood,
you have no life in you.
Anyone who does eat my flesh and drink my blood
has eternal life,
and I shall raise that person up on the last day.
For my flesh is real food
and my blood is real drink.
Whoever eats my flesh and drinks my blood
lives in me
and I live in that person.
As the living Father sent me
and I draw life from the Father,
so whoever eats me will also draw life from me.
This is the bread which has come down from heaven;
it is not like the bread our ancestors ate:
they are dead,
but anyone who eats this bread will live for ever.

This is what he taught at Capernaum in the synagogue. After hearing it, many of his followers said, 'This is intolerable language. How could anyone accept it?' Jesus was aware that his followers were complaining about it and said, 'Does this disturb you? What if you should see the Son of man ascend to where he was before?'

> It is the spirit that gives life,
> the flesh has nothing to offer.
> The words I have spoken to you are spirit
> and they are life.

'But there are some of you who do not believe.' For Jesus knew from the outset who did not believe and who was to betray him. He went on, 'This is why I told you that no one could come to me except by the gift of the Father.' After this, many of his disciples went away and accompanied him no more.

Then Jesus said to the Twelve, 'What about you, do you want to go away too?' Simon Peter answered, 'Lord, to whom shall we go? You have the message of eternal life, and we believe; we have come to know that you are the Holy One of God.' Jesus replied to them, 'Did I not choose the Twelve of you? Yet one of you is a devil.' He meant Judas son of Simon Iscariot, since this was the man, one of the Twelve, who was to betray him.

## JESUS TEACHES IN THE TEMPLE
John 7:1 – 8:1

After this Jesus travelled round Galilee; he could not travel round Judea, because the Jews were seeking to kill him.

As the Jewish feast of Shelters drew near, his brothers said to him, 'Leave this place and go to Judea, so that your disciples, too, can see the works you are doing; no one who wants to be publicly known acts in secret; if this is what you are doing, you should reveal yourself to the world.' Not even his brothers had faith in him. Jesus answered, 'For me the right time has not come yet, but for you any time is the right time. The world cannot hate you, but it does hate me, because

I give evidence that its ways are evil. Go up to the festival yourselves: I am not going to this festival, because for me the time is not ripe yet.' Having said that, he stayed behind in Galilee.

However, after his brothers had left for the festival, he went up as well, not publicly but secretly. At the festival the Jews were on the look-out for him: 'Where is he?' they said. There was a great deal of talk about him in the crowds. Some said, 'He is a good man'; others, 'No, he is leading the people astray.' Yet no one spoke about him openly, for fear of the Jews.

When the festival was half over, Jesus went to the Temple and began to teach. The Jews were astonished and said, 'How did he learn to read? He has not been educated.' Jesus answered them:

> My teaching is not from myself:
> it comes from the one who sent me;
> anyone who is prepared to do his will,
> will know whether my teaching is from God
> or whether I speak on my own account.
> When someone speaks on his own account,
> he is seeking honour for himself;
> but when he is seeking the honour of the person who sent him,
> then he is true
> and altogether without dishonesty.
> Did not Moses give you the Law?
> And yet not one of you keeps the Law!

'Why do you want to kill me?' The crowd replied, 'You are mad! Who wants to kill you?' Jesus answered, 'One work I did, and you are all amazed at it. Moses ordered you to practise circumcision – not that it began with him, it goes back to the patriarchs – and you circumcize on the Sabbath. Now if someone can be circumcized on the Sabbath so that the Law of Moses is not broken, why are you angry with me for making someone completely healthy on a Sabbath? Do not keep judging according to appearances; let your judgment be according to what is right.'

Meanwhile some of the people of Jerusalem were saying, 'Isn't this the man they want to kill? And here he is, speaking openly, and they have nothing to say to him! Can it be true the authorities have recognized that he is the Christ? Yet we all know where he comes from, but when the Christ appears no one will know where he comes from.'

Then, as Jesus was teaching in the Temple, he cried out:

You know me and you know where I came from.
Yet I have not come of my own accord:
but he who sent me is true;
You do not know him,
but I know him
because I have my being from him
and it was he who sent me.

They wanted to arrest him then, but because his hour had not yet come no one laid a hand on him.

There were many people in the crowds, however, who believed in him; they were saying, 'When the Christ comes, will he give more signs than this man has?' Hearing that talk like this about him was spreading among the people, the Pharisees sent the Temple guards to arrest him.

Then Jesus said:

For a short time I am with you still;
then I shall go back to the one who sent me.
You will look for me and will not find me;
where I am
you cannot come.

So the Jews said to one another, 'Where is he intending to go that we shall not be able to find him? Is he intending to go abroad to the people who are dispersed among the Greeks and to teach the Greeks? What does he mean when he says:

You will look for me and will not find me;
where I am,
you cannot come?"'

On the last day, the great day of the festival, Jesus stood and cried out:

Let anyone who is thirsty come to me!
Let anyone who believes in me come and drink!

'As scripture says, "From his heart shall flow streams of living water."'

He was speaking of the Spirit which those who believed in him were to receive; for there was no Spirit as yet because Jesus had not yet been glorified.

Some of the crowd who had been listening said, 'He is indeed the prophet,' and some said, 'He is the Christ,' but others said, 'Would the Christ come from Galilee? Does not scripture say that the Christ must be descended from David and come from Bethlehem, the village where David was?' So the people could not agree about him. Some wanted to arrest him, but no one actually laid a hand on him.

The guards went back to the chief priests and Pharisees who said to them, 'Why haven't you brought him?' The guards replied, 'No one has ever spoken like this man.' 'So,' the Pharisees answered, 'you, too, have been led astray? Have any of the authorities come to believe in him? Any of the Pharisees? This rabble knows nothing about the Law – they are damned.' One of them, Nicodemus – the same man who had come to Jesus earlier – said to them, 'But surely our Law does not allow us to pass judgment on anyone without first giving him a hearing and discovering what he is doing?' To this they answered, 'Are you a Galilean too? Go into the matter, and see for yourself: prophets do not arise in Galilee.'

They all went home, and Jesus went to the Mount of Olives.

## THE WOMAN TAKEN IN ADULTERY
John 8:2–11

At daybreak he appeared in the Temple again; and as all the people came to him, he sat down and began to teach them.

The scribes and Pharisees brought a woman along who had been caught committing adultery; and making her stand there in the middle they said to Jesus, 'Master, this woman was caught in the very

115

act of committing adultery, and in the Law Moses has ordered us to stone women of this kind. What have you got to say?' They asked him this as a test, looking for an accusation to use against him. But Jesus bent down and started writing on the ground with his finger. As they persisted with their question, he straightened up and said, 'Let the one among you who is guiltless be the first to throw a stone at her.' Then he bent down and continued writing on the ground. When they heard this they went away one by one, beginning with the eldest, until the last one had gone and Jesus was left alone with the woman, who remained in the middle. Jesus again straightened up and said, 'Woman, where are they? Has no one condemned you?' 'No one, sir,' she replied. 'Neither do I condemn you,' said Jesus. 'Go away, and from this moment sin no more.'

## 'THE TRUTH WILL SET YOU FREE'
### John 8:12–59

When Jesus spoke to the people again, he said:

> I am the light of the world;
> anyone who follows me will not be walking in the dark
> but will have the light of life.

At this the Pharisees said to him, 'You are testifying on your own behalf; your testimony is not true.' Jesus replied:

> Even though I am testifying on my own behalf,
> my testimony is still true,
> because I know
> where I have come from and where I am going;
> but you do not know
> where I come from or where I am going.
> You judge by human standards;
> I judge no one,
> but if I judge,
> my judgment will be true,
> because I am not alone:

the one who sent me is with me;
and in your Law it is written
that the testimony of two witnesses is true.
I testify on my own behalf,
but the Father who sent me testifies on my behalf, too.

They asked him, 'Where is your Father then?' Jesus answered:

You do not know me, nor do you know my Father;
if you did know me, you would know my Father as well.

He spoke these words in the Treasury, while teaching in the Temple.
No one arrested him, because his hour had not yet come.
Again he said to them:

I am going away; you will look for me
and you will die in your sin.
Where I am going, you cannot come.

So the Jews said to one another, 'Is he going to kill himself, that he
says, "Where I am going, you cannot come?"' Jesus went on:

You are from below;
I am from above.
You are of this world;
I am not of this world.
I have told you already: You will die in your sins.
Yes, if you do not believe that I am He,
you will die in your sins.

So they said to him, 'Who are you?' Jesus answered:

What I have told you from the outset.
About you I have much to say
and much to judge;
but the one who sent me is true,
and what I declare to the world
I have learnt from him.

They did not recognize that he was talking to them about the Father.
So Jesus said:

> When you have lifted up the Son of man,
> then you will know that I am He
> and that I do nothing of my own accord.
> What I say
> is what the Father has taught me;
> he who sent me is with me,
> and has not left me to myself,
> for I always do what pleases him.

As he was saying this, many came to believe in him.
　　To the Jews who believed in him Jesus said:

> If you make my word your home
> you will indeed be my disciples;
> you will come to know the truth,
> and the truth will set you free.

They answered, 'We are descended from Abraham and we have never
been the slaves of anyone; what do you mean, "You will be set free?"'
Jesus replied:

> In all truth I tell you,
> everyone who commits sin is a slave.
> Now a slave has no permanent standing in the household,
> but a son belongs to it for ever.
> So if the Son sets you free,
> you will indeed be free.
> I know that you are descended from Abraham;
> but you want to kill me
> because my word finds no place in you.
> What I speak of
> is what I have seen at my Father's side,
> and you too put into action
> the lessons you have learnt from your father.

They repeated, 'Our father is Abraham.' Jesus said to them:

> If you are Abraham's children,
> do as Abraham did.
> As it is, you want to kill me,
> a man who has told you the truth
> as I have learnt it from God;
> that is not what Abraham did.
> You are doing your father's work.

They replied, 'We were not born illegitimate, the only father we have is God.' Jesus answered:

> If God were your father, you would love me,
> since I have my origin in God and have come from him;
> I did not come of my own accord,
> but he sent me.
> Why do you not understand what I say?
> Because you cannot bear to listen to my words.
> You are from your father, the devil,
> and you prefer to do
> what your father wants.
> He was a murderer from the start;
> he was never grounded in the truth;
> there is no truth in him at all.
> When he lies
> he is speaking true to his nature,
> because he is a liar, and the father of lies.
> But it is because I speak the truth
> that you do not believe me.
> Can any of you convict me of sin?
> If I speak the truth, why do you not believe me?
> Whoever comes from God
> listens to the words of God;
> the reason why you do not listen
> is that you are not from God.

The Jews replied, 'Are we not right in saying that you are a Samaritan and possessed by a devil?' Jesus answered:

> I am not possessed;
> but I honour my Father,
> and you deny me honour.
> I do not seek my own glory;
> there is someone who does seek it and is the judge of it.
> In all truth I tell you,
> whoever keeps my word
> will never see death.

The Jews said, 'Now we know that you are possessed. Abraham is dead, and the prophets are dead, and yet you say, "Whoever keeps my word will never know the taste of death." Are you greater than our father Abraham, who is dead? The prophets are dead too. Who are you claiming to be?' Jesus answered:

> If I were to seek my own glory
> my glory would be worth nothing;
> in fact, my glory is conferred by the Father,
> by the one of whom you say, 'He is our God,'
> although you do not know him.
> But I know him,
> and if I were to say, 'I do not know him,'
> I should be a liar, as you yourselves are.
> But I do know him, and I keep his word.
> Your father Abraham rejoiced
> to think that he would see my Day;
> he saw it and was glad.

The Jews then said, 'You are not fifty yet, and you have seen Abraham!' Jesus replied:

> In all truth I tell you,
> before Abraham ever was,
> I am.

At this they picked up stones to throw at him; but Jesus hid himself and left the Temple.

## THE FIFTH SIGN: JESUS HEALS A MAN BORN BLIND
### John 9

As he went along, he saw a man who had been blind from birth. His disciples asked him, 'Rabbi, who sinned, this man or his parents, that he should have been born blind?' 'Neither he nor his parents sinned,' Jesus answered, 'he was born blind so that the works of God might be revealed in him.'

> As long as day lasts
> we must carry out the work of the one who sent me;
> the night will soon be here when no one can work.
> As long as I am in the world
> I am the light of the world.

Having said this, he spat on the ground, made a paste with the spittle, put this over the eyes of the blind man, and said to him, 'Go and wash in the Pool of Siloam' (the name means 'one who has been sent'). So he went off and washed and came back able to see.

His neighbours and the people who used to see him before (for he was a beggar) said, 'Isn't this the man who used to sit and beg?' Some said, 'Yes, it is the same one.' Others said, 'No, but he looks just like him.' The man himself said, 'Yes, I am the one.' So they said to him, 'Then how is it that your eyes were opened?' He answered, 'The man called Jesus made a paste, daubed my eyes with it and said to me, "Go off and wash at Siloam"; so I went, and when I washed I gained my sight.' They asked, 'Where is he?' He answered, 'I don't know.'

They brought to the Pharisees the man who had been blind. It had been a Sabbath day when Jesus made the paste and opened the man's eyes, so when the Pharisees asked him how he had gained his sight, he said, 'He put a paste on my eyes, and I washed, and I can see.' Then some of the Pharisees said, 'That man cannot be from God:

he does not keep the Sabbath.' Others said, 'How can a sinner produce signs like this?' And there was division among them. So they spoke to the blind man again, 'What have you to say about him yourself, now that he has opened your eyes?' The man answered, 'He is a prophet.'

However, the Jews would not believe that the man had been blind without first sending for the parents of the man who had gained his sight and asking them, 'Is this man really the son of yours who you say was born blind? If so, how is it that he is now able to see?' His parents answered, 'We know he is our son and we know he was born blind, but how he can see, we don't know, nor who opened his eyes. Ask him. He is old enough: let him speak for himself.' His parents spoke like this out of fear of the Jews, who had already agreed to ban from the synagogue anyone who should acknowledge Jesus as the Christ. This was why his parents said, 'He is old enough; ask him.'

So the Jews sent for the man again and said to him, 'Give glory to God! We are satisfied that this man is a sinner.' The man answered, 'Whether he is a sinner I don't know; all I know is that I was blind and now I can see.' They said to him, 'What did he do to you? How did he open your eyes?' He replied, 'I have told you once and you wouldn't listen. Why do you want to hear it all again? Do you want to become his disciples yourselves?' At this they hurled abuse at him, 'It is you who are his disciple, we are disciples of Moses: we know that God spoke to Moses, but as for this man, we don't know where he comes from.' The man replied, 'That is just what is so amazing! You don't know where he comes from and he has opened my eyes! We know that God doesn't listen to sinners, but God does listen to people who are devout and do his will. Ever since the world began it is unheard of for anyone to open the eyes of someone born blind; if this man were not from God, he wouldn't have been able to do anything.' They retorted, 'Are you trying to teach us, and you a sinner through and through ever since you were born!' And they ejected him.

Jesus heard they had ejected him, and when he found him he said to him, 'Do you believe in the Son of man?' 'Sir,' the man replied, 'tell me who he is so that I may believe in him.' Jesus said, 'You have seen him; he is speaking to you.' The man said, 'Lord, I believe,' and worshipped him.

Jesus said:

It is for judgment
that I have come into this world,
so that those without sight may see
and those with sight may become blind.

Hearing this, some Pharisees who were present said to him, 'So we are blind, are we?' Jesus replied:

If you were blind,
you would not be guilty,
but since you say, 'We can see,'
your guilt remains.

## THE GOOD SHEPHERD
### John 10

'In all truth I tell you, anyone who does not enter the sheepfold through the gate, but climbs in some other way, is a thief and a bandit. He who enters through the gate is the shepherd of the flock; the gatekeeper lets him in, the sheep hear his voice, one by one he calls his own sheep and leads them out. When he has brought out all those that are his, he goes ahead of them, and the sheep follow because they know his voice. They will never follow a stranger, but will run away from him because they do not recognize the voice of strangers.'

Jesus told them this parable but they failed to understand what he was saying to them.

So Jesus spoke to them again:

In all truth I tell you,
I am the gate of the sheepfold.
All who have come before me
are thieves and bandits,
but the sheep took no notice of them.
I am the gate.

Anyone who enters through me will be safe:
such a one will go in and out
and will find pasture.
The thief comes
only to steal and kill and destroy.
I have come
so that they may have life
and have it to the full.
I am the good shepherd:
the good shepherd lays down his life for his sheep.
The hired man, since he is not the shepherd
and the sheep do not belong to him,
abandons the sheep
as soon as he sees a wolf coming, and runs away,
and then the wolf attacks and scatters the sheep;
he runs away because he is only a hired man
and has no concern for the sheep.
I am the good shepherd;
I know my own
and my own know me,
just as the Father knows me
and I know the Father;
and I lay down my life for my sheep.
And there are other sheep I have
that are not of this fold,
and I must lead these too.
They too will listen to my voice,
and there will be only one flock,
one shepherd.
The Father loves me,
because I lay down my life
in order to take it up again.
No one takes it from me;
I lay it down of my own free will,
and as I have power to lay it down,
so I have power to take it up again;
and this is the command I have received from my Father.

These words caused a fresh division among the Jews. Many said, 'He is possessed, he is raving; why do you listen to him?' Others said, 'These are not the words of a man possessed by a devil: could a devil open the eyes of the blind?'

It was the time of the feast of Dedication in Jerusalem. It was winter, and Jesus was in the Temple walking up and down in the Portico of Solomon. The Jews gathered round him and said, 'How much longer are you going to keep us in suspense? If you are the Christ, tell us openly.' Jesus replied:

I have told you, but you do not believe.
The works I do in my Father's name are my witness;
but you do not believe,
because you are no sheep of mine.
The sheep that belong to me listen to my voice;
I know them and they follow me.
I give them eternal life;
they will never be lost
and no one will ever steal them from my hand.
The Father, for what he has given me, is greater than anyone,
and no one can steal anything from the Father's hand.
The Father and I are one.

The Jews fetched stones to stone him, so Jesus said to them, 'I have shown you many good works from my Father; for which of these are you stoning me?' The Jews answered him, 'We are stoning you, not for doing a good work, but for blasphemy; though you are only a man, you claim to be God.' Jesus answered:

Is it not written in your Law:
'I said, you are gods?'
So it uses the word 'gods'
of those people to whom the word of God was addressed
– and scripture cannot be set aside.
Yet to someone whom the Father has consecrated
and sent into the world you say,
'You are blaspheming'
because I said, 'I am Son of God.'

If I am not doing my Father's work,
there is no need to believe me;
but if I am doing it,
then even if you refuse to believe in me,
at least believe in the work I do;
then you will know for certain
that the Father is in me and I am in the Father.

They again wanted to arrest him then, but he eluded their clutches.

He went back again to the far side of the Jordan to the district where John had been baptizing at first and he stayed there. Many people who came to him said, 'John gave no signs, but all he said about this man was true'; and many of them believed in him.

## THE SIXTH SIGN: THE RAISING OF LAZARUS
### John 11

There was a man named Lazarus of Bethany, the village of Mary and her sister, Martha, and he was ill. It was the same Mary, the sister of the sick man Lazarus, who anointed the Lord with ointment and wiped his feet with her hair. The sisters sent this message to Jesus, 'Lord, the man you love is ill.' On receiving the message, Jesus said, 'This sickness will not end in death, but it is for God's glory so that through it the Son of God may be glorified.'

Jesus loved Martha and her sister and Lazarus, yet when he heard that he was ill he stayed where he was for two more days before saying to the disciples, 'Let us go back to Judea.' The disciples said, 'Rabbi, it is not long since the Jews were trying to stone you; are you going back there again?' Jesus replied:

Are there not twelve hours in the day?
No one who walks in the daytime stumbles,
having the light of this world to see by;
anyone who walks around at night stumbles,
having no light as a guide.

He said that and then added, 'Our friend Lazarus is at rest; I am going to wake him.' The disciples said to him, 'Lord, if he is at rest he will be saved.' Jesus was speaking of the death of Lazarus, but they thought that by 'rest' he meant 'sleep'; so Jesus put it plainly, 'Lazarus is dead; and for your sake I am glad I was not there because now you will believe. But let us go to him.' Then Thomas – known as the Twin – said to the other disciples, 'Let us also go to die with him.'

On arriving, Jesus found that Lazarus had been in the tomb for four days already. Bethany is only about two miles from Jerusalem, and many Jews had come to Martha and Mary to comfort them about their brother. When Martha heard that Jesus was coming she went to meet him. Mary remained sitting in the house. Martha said to Jesus, 'Lord, if you had been here, my brother would not have died, but even now I know that God will grant whatever you ask of him.' Jesus said to her, 'Your brother will rise again.' Martha said, 'I know he will rise again at the resurrection on the last day.' Jesus said:

I am the resurrection.
Anyone who believes in me, even though that person dies,
    will live,
and whoever lives and believes in me
will never die.
Do you believe this?

'Yes, Lord,' she said, 'I believe that you are the Christ, the Son of God, the one who was to come into this world.'

When she had said this, she went and called her sister Mary, saying in a low voice, 'The Master is here and wants to see you.' Hearing this, Mary got up quickly and went to him. Jesus had not yet come into the village; he was still at the place where Martha had met him. When the Jews who were in the house comforting Mary saw her get up so quickly and go out, they followed her, thinking that she was going to the tomb to weep there.

Mary went to Jesus, and as soon as she saw him she threw herself at his feet, saying, 'Lord, if you had been here, my brother would not have died.' At the sight of her tears, and those of the Jews who had come with her, Jesus was greatly distressed, and with a profound sigh he said, 'Where have you put him?' They said, 'Lord, come and see.' Jesus wept; and the Jews said, 'See how much he loved him!' But there were some who remarked, 'He opened the eyes of the blind man. Could he not have prevented this man's death?' Sighing again, Jesus reached the tomb: it was a cave with a stone to close the opening. Jesus said, 'Take the stone away.' Martha, the dead man's sister, said to him, 'Lord, by now he will smell; this is the fourth day since he died.' Jesus replied, 'Have I not told you that if you believe you will see the glory of God?' So they took the stone away. Then Jesus lifted up his eyes and said:

> Father, I thank you for hearing my prayer.
> I myself knew that you hear me always,
> but I speak
> for the sake of all these who are standing around me,
> so that they may believe it was you who sent me.

When he had said this, he cried in a loud voice, 'Lazarus, come out!' The dead man came out, his feet and hands bound with strips of material, and a cloth over his face. Jesus said to them, 'Unbind him, let him go free.'

Many of the Jews who had come to visit Mary, and had seen what he did, believed in him, but some of them went to the Pharisees to tell them what Jesus had done. Then the chief priests and Pharisees called a meeting. 'Here is this man working all these signs,' they said, 'and what action are we taking? If we let him go on in this way everybody will believe in him, and the Romans will come and suppress the Holy Place and our nation.' One of them, Caiaphas, the high priest that year, said, 'You do not seem to have grasped the situation at all; you fail to see that it is to your advantage that one man should die for the people, rather than that the whole nation should perish.'

He did not speak in his own person, but as high priest of that year he was prophesying that Jesus was to die for the nation – and not for the nation only, but also to gather together into one the scattered children of God. From that day onwards they were determined to kill him. So Jesus no longer went about openly among the Jews, but left the district for a town called Ephraim, in the country bordering on the desert, and stayed there with his disciples.

The Jewish Passover was drawing near, and many of the country people who had gone up to Jerusalem before the Passover to purify themselves were looking out for Jesus, saying to one another as they stood about in the Temple, 'What do you think? Will he come to the festival or not?' The chief priests and Pharisees had by now given their orders: anyone who knew where he was must inform them so that they could arrest him.

## Part Two

# The Darkness Defeated

## MARY ANOINTS JESUS
### John 12:1–11

Six days before the Passover, Jesus went to Bethany, where Lazarus was, whom he had raised from the dead. They gave a dinner for him there; Martha waited on them and Lazarus was among those at table. Mary brought in a pound of very costly ointment, pure nard, and with it anointed the feet of Jesus, wiping them with her hair; the house was filled with the scent of the ointment. Then Judas Iscariot – one of his disciples, the man who was to betray him – said, 'Why was this ointment not sold for three hundred denarii and the money given to the poor?' He said this, not because he cared about the poor, but because he was a thief; he was in charge of the common fund and used to help himself to the contents. So Jesus said, 'Leave her alone; let her keep it for the day of my burial. You have the poor with you always, you will not always have me.'

Meanwhile a large number of Jews heard that he was there and came not only on account of Jesus but also to see Lazarus whom he had raised from the dead. Then the chief priests decided to kill Lazarus as well, since it was on his account that many of the Jews were leaving them and believing in Jesus.

## JESUS ENTERS JERUSALEM
### John 12:12–50

The next day the great crowd of people who had come up for the festival heard that Jesus was on his way to Jerusalem. They took branches of palm and went out to receive him, shouting:

Hosanna!
Blessed is he who is coming in the name of the Lord,
the king of Israel.

Jesus found a young donkey and mounted it – as scripture says:

Do not be afraid, daughter of Zion;
look, your king is approaching,
riding on the foal of a donkey.

At first his disciples did not understand this, but later, after Jesus had been glorified, they remembered that this had been written about him and that this was what had happened to him. The crowd who had been with him when he called Lazarus out of the tomb and raised him from the dead kept bearing witness to it; this was another reason why the crowd came out to receive him: they had heard that he had given this sign. Then the Pharisees said to one another, 'You see, you are making no progress; look, the whole world has gone after him!'

Among those who went up to worship at the festival were some Greeks. These approached Philip, who came from Bethsaida in Galilee, and put this request to him, 'Sir, we should like to see Jesus.' Philip went to tell Andrew, and Andrew and Philip together went to tell Jesus.

Jesus replied to them:

Now the hour has come
for the Son of man to be glorified.
In all truth I tell you,
unless a wheat grain falls into the earth and dies,
it remains only a single grain;
but if it dies
it yields a rich harvest.
Anyone who loves his life loses it;
anyone who hates his life in this world
will keep it for eternal life.
Whoever serves me, must follow me,
and my servant will be with me wherever I am.
If anyone serves me, my Father will honour him.

Now my soul is troubled.
What shall I say:
Father, save me from this hour?
But it is for this very reason that I have come to this hour.
Father, glorify your name!

A voice came from heaven, 'I have glorified it, and I will again glorify it.'

The crowd standing by, who heard this, said it was a clap of thunder; others said, 'It was an angel speaking to him.' Jesus answered, 'It was not for my sake that this voice came, but for yours.'

Now sentence is being passed on this world;
now the prince of this world is to be driven out.
And when I am lifted up from the earth,
I shall draw all people to myself.

By these words he indicated the kind of death he would die. The crowd answered, 'The Law has taught us that the Christ will remain for ever. So how can you say, "The Son of man must be lifted up"? Who is this Son of man?' Jesus then said:

The light will be with you only a little longer now.
Go on your way while you have the light,
or darkness will overtake you,
and nobody who walks in the dark knows where he is going.
While you still have the light,
believe in the light
so that you may become children of light.

Having said this, Jesus left them and was hidden from their sight.

Though they had been present when he gave so many signs, they did not believe in him; this was to fulfil the words of the prophet Isaiah:

Lord, who has given credence to what they have heard from us,
and who has seen in it a revelation of the Lord's arm?

Indeed, they were unable to believe because, as Isaiah says again:

> He has blinded their eyes,
> he has hardened their heart,
> to prevent them from using their eyes to see,
> using their heart to understand,
> changing their ways and being healed by me.

Isaiah said this because he saw his glory, and his words referred to Jesus.

And yet there were many who did believe in him, even among the leading men, but they did not admit it, because of the Pharisees and for fear of being banned from the synagogue: they put human glory before God's glory.

Jesus declared publicly:

> Whoever believes in me
> believes not in me
> but in the one who sent me,
> and whoever sees me,
> sees the one who sent me.
> I have come into the world as light,
> to prevent anyone who believes in me
> from staying in the dark any more.
> If anyone hears my words and does not keep them faithfully,
> it is not I who shall judge such a person,
> since I have come not to judge the world,
> but to save the world:
> anyone who rejects me and refuses my words
> has his judge already:
> the word itself that I have spoken
> will be his judge on the last day.
> For I have not spoken of my own accord;
> but the Father who sent me
> commanded me what to say and what to speak,
> and I know that his commands mean eternal life.
> And therefore what the Father has told me
> is what I speak.

# JESUS WASHES HIS DISCIPLES' FEET
John 13:1–30

Before the festival of the Passover, Jesus, knowing that his hour had come to pass from this world to the Father, having loved those who were his in the world, loved them to the end.

They were at supper, and the devil had already put it into the mind of Judas Iscariot son of Simon, to betray him. Jesus knew that the Father had put everything into his hands, and that he had come from God and was returning to God, and he got up from table, removed his outer garments and, taking a towel, wrapped it round his waist; he then poured water into a basin and began to wash the disciples' feet and to wipe them with the towel he was wearing.

He came to Simon Peter, who said to him, 'Lord, are you going to wash my feet?' Jesus answered, 'At the moment you do not know what I am doing, but later you will understand.' 'Never!' said Peter, 'You shall never wash my feet.' Jesus replied, 'If I do not wash you, you can have no share with me.' Simon Peter said, 'Well then, Lord, not only my feet, but my hands and my head as well!' Jesus said, 'No one who has had a bath needs washing, such a person is clean all over. You too are clean, though not all of you are.' He knew who was going to betray him, and that was why he said, 'though not all of you are'.

When he had washed their feet and put on his outer garments again he went back to the table. 'Do you understand', he said, 'what I have done to you? You call me Master and Lord, and rightly; so I am. If I, then, the Lord and Master, have washed your feet, you must wash each other's feet. I have given you an example so that you may copy what I have done to you.'

In all truth I tell you,
no servant is greater than his master,
no messenger is greater than the one who sent him.

'Now that you know this, blessed are you if you behave accordingly. I am not speaking about all of you: I know the ones I have chosen; but what scripture says must be fulfilled:'

He who shares my table
takes advantage of me.
I tell you this now, before it happens,
so that when it does happen
you may believe that I am He.
In all truth I tell you,
whoever welcomes the one I send, welcomes me,
and whoever welcomes me, welcomes the one who sent me.

Having said this, Jesus was deeply disturbed and declared, 'In all truth I tell you, one of you is going to betray me.' The disciples looked at each other, wondering whom he meant. The disciple Jesus loved was reclining next to Jesus; Simon Peter signed to him and said, 'Ask who it is he means,' so leaning back close to Jesus' chest he said, 'Who is it, Lord?' Jesus answered, 'It is the one to whom I give the piece of bread that I dip in the dish.' And when he had dipped the piece of bread he gave it to Judas son of Simon Iscariot. At that instant, after Judas had taken the bread, Satan entered him. Jesus then said, 'What you are going to do, do quickly.' None of the others at table understood why he said this. Since Judas had charge of the common fund, some of them thought Jesus was telling him, 'Buy what we need for the festival,' or telling him to give something to the poor. As soon as Judas had taken the piece of bread he went out. It was night.

### 'LOVE ONE ANOTHER'
John 13:31–38

When he had gone, Jesus said:

Now has the Son of man been glorified,
and in him God has been glorified.
If God has been glorified in him,
God will in turn glorify him in himself,
and will glorify him very soon.
Little children,
I shall be with you only a little longer.

135

You will look for me,
and, as I told the Jews,
where I am going,
you cannot come.
I give you a new commandment:
love one another;
you must love one another
just as I have loved you.
It is by your love for one another,
that everyone will recognize you
as my disciples.

Simon Peter said, 'Lord, where are you going?' Jesus replied, 'Now you cannot follow me where I am going, but later you shall follow me.' Peter said to him, 'Why can I not follow you now? I will lay down my life for you.' 'Lay down your life for me?' answered Jesus. 'In all truth I tell you, before the cock crows you will have disowned me three times.'

## THE WAY, THE TRUTH AND THE LIFE
### John 14

Do not let your hearts be troubled.
You trust in God, trust also in me.
In my Father's house there are many places to live in;
otherwise I would have told you.
I am going now to prepare a place for you,
and after I have gone and prepared you a place,
I shall return to take you to myself,
so that you may be with me
where I am.
You know the way to the place where I am going.

Thomas said, 'Lord, we do not know where you are going, so how can we know the way?' Jesus said:

136

I am the Way; I am Truth and Life.
No one can come to the Father except through me.
If you know me, you will know my Father too.
From this moment you know him and have seen him.

Philip said, 'Lord, show us the Father and then we shall be satisfied.'
Jesus said to him, 'Have I been with you all this time, Philip, and you
still do not know me?

Anyone who has seen me has seen the Father,
so how can you say, 'Show us the Father'?
Do you not believe
that I am in the Father and the Father is in me?
What I say to you I do not speak of my own accord:
it is the Father, living in me, who is doing his works.
You must believe me when I say
that I am in the Father and the Father is in me;
or at least believe it on the evidence of these works.
In all truth I tell you,
whoever believes in me
will perform the same works as I do myself,
and will perform even greater works,
because I am going to the Father.
Whatever you ask in my name I will do,
so that the Father may be glorified in the Son.
If you ask me anything in my name,
I will do it.
If you love me you will keep my commandments.
I shall ask the Father,
and he will give you another Paraclete
to be with you for ever,
the Spirit of truth
whom the world can never accept
since it neither sees nor knows him;
but you know him,
because he is with you, he is in you.
I shall not leave you orphans;

I shall come to you.
In a short time the world will no longer see me;
but you will see that I live
and you also will live.
On that day
you will know that I am in my Father
and you in me and I in you.
Whoever holds to my commandments and keeps them
is the one who loves me;
and whoever loves me will be loved by my Father,
and I shall love him and reveal myself to him.

Judas – not Judas Iscariot – said to him, 'Lord, what has happened, that you intend to show yourself to us and not to the world?' Jesus replied:

Anyone who loves me will keep my word,
and my Father will love him,
and we shall come to him
and make a home in him.
Anyone who does not love me does not keep my words.
And the word that you hear is not my own:
it is the word of the Father who sent me.
I have said these things to you
while still with you;
but the Paraclete, the Holy Spirit,
whom the Father will send in my name,
will teach you everything
and remind you of all I have said to you.
Peace I bequeath to you,
my own peace I give you,
a peace which the world cannot give, this is my gift to you.
Do not let your hearts be troubled or afraid.
You heard me say:
I am going away and shall return.
If you loved me you would be glad that I am going to
    the Father,

for the Father is greater than I.
I have told you this now, before it happens,
so that when it does happen you may believe.
I shall not talk to you much longer,
because the prince of this world is on his way.
He has no power over me,
but the world must recognize that I love the Father
and that I act just as the Father commanded.
Come now, let us go.


# THE TRUE VINE
### John 15:1–16


I am the true vine,
and my Father is the vinedresser.
Every branch in me that bears no fruit
he cuts away,
and every branch that does bear fruit he prunes
to make it bear even more.
You are clean already,
by means of the word that I have spoken to you.
Remain in me, as I in you.
As a branch cannot bear fruit all by itself,
unless it remains part of the vine,
neither can you unless you remain in me.
I am the vine,
you are the branches.
Whoever remains in me, with me in him,
bears fruit in plenty;
for cut off from me you can do nothing.
Anyone who does not remain in me
is thrown away like a branch
– and withers;
these branches are collected and thrown on the fire
and are burnt.

If you remain in me
and my words remain in you,
you may ask for whatever you please
and you will get it.
It is to the glory of my Father that you should bear much fruit
and be my disciples.
I have loved you
just as the Father has loved me.
Remain in my love.
If you keep my commandments
you will remain in my love,
just as I have kept my Father's commandments
and remain in his love.
I have told you this
so that my own joy may be in you
and your joy be complete.
This is my commandment:
love one another,
as I have loved you.
No one can have greater love
than to lay down his life for his friends.
You are my friends,
if you do what I command you.
I shall no longer call you servants,
because a servant does not know
the master's business;
I call you friends,
because I have made known to you
everything I have learnt from my Father.
You did not choose me,
no, I chose you;
and I commissioned you
to go out and to bear fruit,
fruit that will last;
so that the Father will give you
anything you ask him in my name.

# 'I HAVE CONQUERED THE WORLD'
## John 15:17 – 16:33

My command to you
is to love one another.
If the world hates you,
you must realize that it hated me before it hated you.
If you belonged to the world,
the world would love you as its own;
but because you do not belong to the world,
because my choice of you has drawn you out of the world,
that is why the world hates you.
Remember the words I said to you:
A servant is not greater than his master.
If they persecuted me,
they will persecute you too;
if they kept my word,
they will keep yours as well.
But it will be on my account that they will do all this to you,
because they do not know the one who sent me.
If I had not come,
if I had not spoken to them,
they would have been blameless;
but as it is they have no excuse for their sin.
Anyone who hates me hates my Father.
If I had not performed such works among them
as no one else has ever done,
they would be blameless;
but as it is, in spite of what they have seen,
they hate both me and my Father.
But all this was only to fulfil the words written in their Law:
'They hated me without reason'.
When the Paraclete comes,
whom I shall send to you from the Father,
the Spirit of truth who issues from the Father,
he will be my witness.

And you too will be witnesses,
because you have been with me from the beginning.
I have told you all this
so that you may not fall away.
They will expel you from the synagogues,
and indeed the time is coming
when anyone who kills you will think he is doing a holy
    service to God.
They will do these things
because they have never known either the Father or me.
But I have told you all this,
so that when the time for it comes
you may remember that I told you.

I did not tell you this from the beginning,
because I was with you;
but now I am going to the one who sent me.
Not one of you asks, 'Where are you going?'
Yet you are sad at heart because I have told you this.
Still, I am telling you the truth:
it is for your own good that I am going,
because unless I go, the Paraclete will not come to you;
but if I go, I will send him to you.
And when he comes,
he will show the world how wrong it was,
about sin,
and about who was in the right,
and about judgment:
about sin:
in that they refuse to believe in me;
about who was in the right:
in that I am going to the Father
and you will see me no more;
about judgment:
in that the prince of this world is already condemned.
I still have many things to say to you
but they would be too much for you to bear now.

However, when the Spirit of truth comes
he will lead you to the complete truth,
since he will not be speaking of his own accord,
but will say only what he has been told;
and he will reveal to you the things to come.
He will glorify me,
since all he reveals to you
will be taken from what is mine.
Everything the Father has is mine;
that is why I said:
all he reveals to you
will be taken from what is mine.

In a short time you will no longer see me,
and then a short time later you will see me again.

Then some of his disciples said to one another, 'What does he mean,
"In a short time you will no longer see me, and then a short time later
you will see me again," and, "I am going to the Father"? What is this
"short time"? We don't know what he means.' Jesus knew that they
wanted to question him, so he said, 'You are asking one another what
I meant by saying, "In a short time you will no longer see me, and
then a short time later you will see me again."'

In all truth I tell you,
you will be weeping and wailing
while the world will rejoice;
you will be sorrowful,
but your sorrow will turn to joy.
A woman in childbirth suffers,
because her time has come;
but when she has given birth to the child she forgets the
     suffering
in her joy that a human being has been born into the world.
So it is with you: you are sad now,
but I shall see you again, and your hearts will be full of joy,
and that joy no one shall take from you.

When that day comes,
you will not ask me any questions.
In all truth I tell you,
anything you ask from the Father
he will grant in my name.
Until now you have not asked anything in my name.
Ask and you will receive,
and so your joy will be complete.
I have been telling you these things in veiled language.
The hour is coming
when I shall no longer speak to you in veiled language
but tell you about the Father in plain words.
When that day comes
you will ask in my name;
and I do not say that I shall pray to the Father for you,
because the Father himself loves you
for loving me,
and believing that I came from God.
I came from the Father and have come into the world
and now I am leaving the world to go to the Father.

His disciples said, 'Now you are speaking plainly and not using veiled language. Now we see that you know everything and need not wait for questions to be put into words; because of this we believe that you came from God.' Jesus answered them:

Do you believe at last?
Listen; the time will come – indeed it has come already –
when you are going to be scattered, each going his own way
and leaving me alone.
And yet I am not alone,
because the Father is with me.
I have told you all this
so that you may find peace in me.
In the world you will have hardship,
but be courageous:
I have conquered the world.

## JESUS PRAYS FOR HIS DISCIPLES
John 17

After saying this, Jesus raised his eyes to heaven and said:

Father, the hour has come:
glorify your Son
so that your Son may glorify you;
so that, just as you have given him power over all humanity,
he may give eternal life to all those you have entrusted to him.
And eternal life is this:
to know you,
the only true God,
and Jesus Christ whom you have sent.
I have glorified you on earth
by finishing the work
that you gave me to do.
Now, Father, glorify me
with that glory I had with you
before ever the world existed.
I have revealed your name
to those whom you took from the world to give me.
They were yours and you gave them to me,
and they have kept your word.
Now at last they have recognized
that all you have given me comes from you
for I have given them
the teaching you gave to me,
and they have indeed accepted it
and know for certain that I came from you,
and have believed that it was you who sent me.
It is for them that I pray.
I am not praying for the world
but for those you have given me,
because they belong to you.
All I have is yours
and all you have is mine,

and in them I am glorified.
I am no longer in the world,
but they are in the world,
and I am coming to you.
Holy Father,
keep those you have given me true to your name,
so that they may be one like us.
While I was with them,
I kept those you had given me true to your name.
I have watched over them and not one is lost
except one who was destined to be lost,
and this was to fulfil the scriptures.
But now I am coming to you
and I say these things in the world
to share my joy with them to the full.
I passed your word on to them,
and the world hated them,
because they belong to the world
no more than I belong to the world.
I am not asking you to remove them from the world,
but to protect them from the Evil One.
They do not belong to the world
any more than I belong to the world.
Consecrate them in the truth;
your word is truth.
As you sent me into the world,
I have sent them into the world,
and for their sake I consecrate myself
so that they too may be consecrated in truth.
I pray not only for these
but also for those
who through their teaching will come to believe in me.
May they all be one,
just as, Father, you are in me and I am in you,
so that they also may be in us,
so that the world may believe it was you who sent me.
I have given them the glory you gave to me,

that they may be one as we are one.
With me in them and you in me,
may they be so perfected in unity
that the world will recognize that it was you who sent me
and that you have loved them as you have loved me.

Father,
I want those you have given me
to be with me where I am,
so that they may always see my glory
which you have given me
because you loved me
before the foundation of the world.
Father, Upright One,
the world has not known you,
but I have known you,
and these have known
that you have sent me.
I have made your name known to them
and will continue to make it known,
so that the love with which you loved me may be in them,
and so that I may be in them.

## JUDAS BETRAYS HIS MASTER
John 18:1–14

After he had said all this, Jesus left with his disciples and crossed the Kidron valley where there was a garden into which he went with his disciples. Judas the traitor knew the place also, since Jesus had often met his disciples there, so Judas brought the cohort to this place together with guards sent by the chief priests and the Pharisees, all with lanterns and torches and weapons. Knowing everything that was to happen to him, Jesus came forward and said, 'Who are you looking for?' They answered, 'Jesus the Nazarene.' He said, 'I am he.' Now Judas the traitor was standing among them. When Jesus said to them,

147

'I am he,' they moved back and fell on the ground. He asked them a second time, 'Who are you looking for?' They said, 'Jesus the Nazarene.' Jesus replied, 'I have told you that I am he. If I am the one you are looking for, let these others go.' This was to fulfil the words he had spoken, 'Not one of those you gave me have I lost.'

Simon Peter, who had a sword, drew it and struck the high priest's servant, cutting off his right ear. The servant's name was Malchus. Jesus said to Peter, 'Put your sword back in its scabbard; am I not to drink the cup that the Father has given me?'

The cohort and its tribune and the Jewish guards seized Jesus and bound him. They took him first to Annas, because Annas was the father-in-law of Caiaphas, who was high priest that year. It was Caiaphas who had counselled the Jews, 'It is better for one man to die for the people.'

## PETER'S DENIAL
### John 18:15–27

Simon Peter, with another disciple, followed Jesus. This disciple, who was known to the high priest, went with Jesus into the high priest's palace, but Peter stayed outside the door. So the other disciple, the one known to the high priest, went out, spoke to the door-keeper and brought Peter in. The girl on duty at the door said to Peter, 'Aren't you another of that man's disciples?' He answered, 'I am not.' Now it was cold, and the servants and guards had lit a charcoal fire and were standing there warming themselves; so Peter stood there too, warming himself with the others.

The high priest questioned Jesus about his disciples and his teaching. Jesus answered, 'I have spoken openly for all the world to hear; I have always taught in the synagogue and in the Temple where all the Jews meet together; I have said nothing in secret. Why ask me? Ask my hearers what I taught; they know what I said.' At these words, one of the guards standing by gave Jesus a slap in the face, saying, 'Is that the way you answer the high priest?' Jesus replied, 'If there is some offence in what I said, point it out; but if not, why do you strike me?' Then Annas sent him, bound, to Caiaphas the high priest.

As Simon Peter stood there warming himself, someone said to him, 'Aren't you another of his disciples?' He denied it saying, 'I am not.' One of the high priest's servants, a relation of the man whose ear Peter had cut off, said, 'Didn't I see you in the garden with him?' Again Peter denied it; and at once a cock crowed.

## THE TRIAL BEFORE PILATE
### John 18:28 – 19:15

They then led Jesus from the house of Caiaphas to the Praetorium. It was now morning. They did not go into the Praetorium themselves to avoid becoming defiled and unable to eat the Passover. So Pilate came outside to them and said, 'What charge do you bring against this man?' They replied, 'If he were not a criminal, we should not have handed him over to you.' Pilate said, 'Take him yourselves, and try him by your own Law.' The Jews answered, 'We are not allowed to put anyone to death.' This was to fulfil the words Jesus had spoken indicating the way he was going to die.

So Pilate went back into the Praetorium and called Jesus to him and asked him, 'Are you the king of the Jews?' Jesus replied, 'Do you ask this of your own accord, or have others said it to you about me?' Pilate answered, 'Am I a Jew? It is your own people and the chief priests who have handed you over to me: what have you done?' Jesus replied, 'Mine is not a kingdom of this world; if my kingdom were of this world, my men would have fought to prevent my being surrendered to the Jews. As it is, my kingdom does not belong here.' Pilate said, 'So, then you are a king?' Jesus answered, 'It is you who say that I am a king. I was born for this, I came into the world for this, to bear witness to the truth; and all who are on the side of truth listen to my voice.' 'Truth?' said Pilate. 'What is that?' And so saying he went out again to the Jews and said, 'I find no case against him. But according to a custom of yours I should release one prisoner at the Passover; would you like me, then, to release for you the king of the Jews?' At this they shouted, 'Not this man,' they said, 'but Barabbas' Barabbas was a bandit.

Pilate then had Jesus taken away and scourged; and after this, the soldiers twisted some thorns into a crown and put it on his head and dressed him in a purple robe. They kept coming up to him and saying, 'Hail, king of the Jews!' and slapping him in the face.

Pilate came outside again and said to them, 'Look, I am going to bring him out to you to let you see that I find no case against him.' Jesus then came out wearing the crown of thorns and the purple robe. Pilate said, 'Here is the man.' When they saw him, the chief priests and the guards shouted, 'Crucify him! Crucify him!' Pilate said, 'Take him yourselves and crucify him: I find no case against him.' The Jews replied, 'We have a Law, and according to that Law he ought to be put to death, because he has claimed to be Son of God.'

When Pilate heard them say this his fears increased. Re-entering the Praetorium, he said to Jesus, 'Where do you come from?' But Jesus made no answer. Pilate then said to him, 'Are you refusing to speak to me? Surely you know I have power to release you and I have power to crucify you?' Jesus replied, 'You would have no power over me at all if it had not been given you from above; that is why the one who handed me over to you has the greater guilt.'

From that moment Pilate was anxious to set him free, but the Jews shouted, 'If you set him free you are no friend of Caesar's; anyone who makes himself king is defying Caesar.' Hearing these words, Pilate had Jesus brought out, and seated him on the chair of judgment at a place called the Pavement, in Hebrew Gabbatha. It was the Day of Preparation, about the sixth hour. 'Here is your king,' said Pilate to the Jews. But they shouted, 'Away with him, away with him, crucify him.' Pilate said, 'Shall I crucify your king?' The chief priests answered, 'We have no king except Caesar.'

## THE CRUCIFIXION
### John 19:16–30

So at that Pilate handed him over to them to be crucified. They then took charge of Jesus, and carrying his own cross he went out to the Place of the Skull or, as it is called in Hebrew, Golgotha, where they crucified him with two others, one on either side, Jesus being in the middle. Pilate wrote out a notice and had it fixed to the cross; it ran

'Jesus the Nazarene, King of the Jews'. This notice was read by many of the Jews, because the place where Jesus was crucified was near the city, and the writing was in Hebrew, Latin and Greek. So the Jewish chief priests said to Pilate, 'You should not write "King of the Jews", but that the man said, "I am King of the Jews".' Pilate answered, 'What I have written, I have written.'

When the soldiers had finished crucifying Jesus they took his clothing and divided it into four shares, one for each soldier. His undergarment was seamless, woven in one piece from neck to hem; so they said to one another, 'Instead of tearing it, let's throw dice to decide who is to have it.' In this way the words of scripture were fulfilled:

> They divide my garments among them
> and cast lots for my clothes.

That is what the soldiers did.

Near the cross of Jesus stood his mother and his mother's sister, Mary the wife of Clopas, and Mary of Magdala. Seeing his mother and the disciple whom he loved standing near her, Jesus said to his mother, 'Woman, this is your son.' Then to the disciple he said, 'This is your mother.' And from that hour the disciple took her into his home.

After this, Jesus knew that everything had now been completed and, so that the scripture should be completely fulfilled, he said:

> I am thirsty.

A jar full of sour wine stood there; so, putting a sponge soaked in the wine on a hyssop stick, they held it up to his mouth. After Jesus had taken the wine he said, 'It is fulfilled'; and bowing his head he gave up his spirit.

## THE ENTOMBMENT
### John 19:31–42

It was the Day of Preparation, and to avoid the bodies' remaining on the cross during the Sabbath – since that Sabbath was a day of special solemnity – the Jews asked Pilate to have the legs broken and the bodies taken away. Consequently the soldiers came and broke the legs of the first man who had been crucified with him and then of the other. When they came to Jesus, they saw he was already dead, and so instead of breaking his legs one of the soldiers pierced his side with a lance; and immediately there came out blood and water. This is the evidence of one who saw it – true evidence, and he knows that what he says is true – and he gives it so that you may believe as well. Because all this happened to fulfil the words of scripture:

Not one bone of his will be broken;

and again, in another place scripture says:

They will look to the one whom they have pierced.

After this, Joseph of Arimathaea, who was a disciple of Jesus – though a secret one because he was afraid of the Jews – asked Pilate to let him remove the body of Jesus. Pilate gave permission, so they came and took it away. Nicodemus came as well – the same one who had first come to Jesus at night-time – and he brought a mixture of myrrh and aloes, weighing about a hundred pounds. They took the body of Jesus and bound it in linen cloths with the spices, following the Jewish burial custom. At the place where he had been crucified there was a garden, and in this garden a new tomb in which no one had yet been buried. Since it was the Jewish Day of Preparation and the tomb was nearby, they laid Jesus there.

## THE RESURRECTION
### John 20

It was very early on the first day of the week and still dark, when Mary of Magdala came to the tomb. She saw that the stone had been moved away from the tomb and came running to Simon Peter and the other disciple, the one whom Jesus loved. 'They have taken the Lord out of the tomb,' she said, 'and we don't know where they have put him.'

So Peter set out with the other disciple to go to the tomb. They ran together, but the other disciple, running faster than Peter, reached the tomb first; he bent down and saw the linen cloths lying on the ground, but did not go in. Simon Peter, following him, also came up, went into the tomb, saw the linen cloths lying on the ground and also the cloth that had been over his head; this was not with the linen cloths but rolled up in a place by itself. Then the other disciple who had reached the tomb first also went in; he saw and he believed. Till this moment they had still not understood the scripture, that he must rise from the dead. The disciples then went back home.

But Mary was standing outside near the tomb, weeping. Then, as she wept, she stooped to look inside, and saw two angels in white sitting where the body of Jesus had been, one at the head, the other at the feet. They said, 'Woman, why are you weeping?' 'They have taken my Lord away,' she replied, 'and I don't know where they have put him.' As she said this she turned round and saw Jesus standing there, though she did not realize that it was Jesus. Jesus said to her, 'Woman, why are you weeping? Who are you looking for?' Supposing him to be the gardener, she said, 'Sir, if you have taken him away, tell me where you have put him, and I will go and remove him.' Jesus said, 'Mary!' She turned round then and said to him in Hebrew, 'Rabbuni!' – which means Master. Jesus said to her, 'Do not cling to me, because I have not yet ascended to the Father. But go to the brothers, and tell them: I am ascending to my Father and your Father, to my God and your God.' So Mary of Magdala told the disciples, 'I have seen the Lord,' and that he had said these things to her.

In the evening of that same day, the first day of the week, the doors were closed in the room where the disciples were, for fear of the Jews. Jesus came and stood among them. He said to them, 'Peace be with you,' and, after saying this, he showed them his hands and his side. The disciples were filled with joy at seeing the Lord, and he said to them again, 'Peace be with you.'

> As the Father sent me,
> so am I sending you.

After saying this he breathed on them and said:

> Receive the Holy Spirit.
> If you forgive anyone's sins,

> they are forgiven;
> if you retain anyone's sins,
> they are retained.

Thomas, called the Twin, who was one of the Twelve, was not with them when Jesus came. So the other disciples said to him, 'We have seen the Lord,' but he answered, 'Unless I can see the holes that the nails made in his hands and can put my finger into the holes they made, and unless I can put my hand into his side, I refuse to believe.' Eight days later the disciples were in the house again and Thomas was with them. The doors were closed, but Jesus came in and stood among them. 'Peace be with you,' he said. Then he spoke to Thomas, 'Put your finger here; look, here are my hands. Give me your hand; put it into my side. Do not be unbelieving any more but believe.' Thomas replied, 'My Lord and my God!' Jesus said to him:

> You believe because you can see me.
> Blessed are those who have not seen and yet believe.

There were many other signs that Jesus worked in the sight of the disciples, but they are not recorded in this book. These are recorded so that you may believe that Jesus is the Christ, the Son of God, and that believing this you may have life through his name.

## EPILOGUE – THE SEVENTH SIGN: JESUS' LAST APPEARANCE TO HIS DISCIPLES
### John 21

Later on, Jesus revealed himself again to the disciples. It was by the Sea of Tiberias, and it happened like this: Simon Peter, Thomas called the Twin, Nathanael from Cana in Galilee, the sons of Zebedee and two more of his disciples were together. Simon Peter said, 'I'm going fishing.' They replied, 'We'll come with you.' They went out and got into the boat but caught nothing that night.

When it was already light, there stood Jesus on the shore, though the disciples did not realize that it was Jesus. Jesus called out,

'Haven't you caught anything, friends?' And when they answered, 'No,' he said, 'Throw the net out to starboard and you'll find something.' So they threw the net out and could not haul it in because of the quantity of fish. The disciple whom Jesus loved said to Peter, 'It is the Lord.' At these words, 'It is the Lord,' Simon Peter tied his outer garment round him (for he had nothing on) and jumped into the water. The other disciples came on in the boat, towing the net with the fish; they were only about a hundred yards from land.

As soon as they came ashore they saw that there was some bread there and a charcoal fire with fish cooking on it. Jesus said, 'Bring some of the fish you have just caught.' Simon Peter went aboard and dragged the net ashore, full of big fish, one hundred and fifty-three of them; and in spite of there being so many the net was not broken. Jesus said to them, 'Come and have breakfast.' None of the disciples was bold enough to ask, 'Who are you?' They knew quite well it was the Lord. Jesus then stepped forward, took the bread and gave it to them, and the same with the fish. This was the third time that Jesus revealed himself to the disciples after rising from the dead.

When they had eaten, Jesus said to Simon Peter, 'Simon son of John, do you love me more than these others do?' He answered, 'Yes, Lord, you know I love you.' Jesus said to him, 'Feed my lambs.' A second time he said to him, 'Simon son of John, do you love me?' He replied, 'Yes, Lord, you know I love you.' Jesus said to him, 'Look after my sheep.' Then he said to him a third time, 'Simon son of John, do you love me?' Peter was hurt that he asked him a third time, 'Do you love me?' and said, 'Lord, you know everything; you know I love you.' Jesus said to him, 'Feed my sheep.'

In all truth I tell you,
when you were young
you put on your own belt
and walked where you liked;
but when you grow old
you will stretch out your hands,
and somebody else will put a belt round you
and take you where you would rather not go.

155

In these words he indicated the kind of death by which Peter would give glory to God. After this he said, 'Follow me.'

Peter turned and saw the disciple whom Jesus loved following them – the one who had leant back close to his chest at the supper and had said to him, 'Lord, who is it that will betray you?' Seeing him, Peter said to Jesus, 'What about him, Lord?' Jesus answered, 'If I want him to stay behind till I come, what does it matter to you? You are to follow me.' The rumour then went out among the brothers that this disciple would not die. Yet Jesus had not said to Peter, 'He will not die,' but, 'If I want him to stay behind till I come.'

This disciple is the one who vouches for these things and has written them down, and we know that his testimony is true.

There was much else that Jesus did; if it were written down in detail, I do not suppose the world itself would hold all the books that would be written.

# Index of Primary Sources

Absire, Alain   56

Aelfric   80

Aelred of Rievaulx   48

Ambrose, St   49

Andrewes, Lancelot   58

Anselm of Canterbury   20

Antoninus, Brother   61

Aquinas, St Thomas   63

Arnold, Matthew   22, 53

Asch, Sholem   71, 83

Augustine, St   26, 27, 36, 49, 58, 69, 71

Avison, Margaret   33

Bacon, Francis   81

Barth, John   45, 66

Bates, Katherine Lee   70

Bede, The Venerable   49

Benedict of Gloucester   50

Bentley, Eric   83

Bernard of Clairvaux, St   58

Bishop, John Peale   60

Blake, William   21, 22, 28, 29, 31,54, 55, 59, 79, 81

Blunt, Hugh   60

Bontemps, Arna   25

Breton, Nicholas   58

Brome, Richard   59

Brontë, Emily   52

Brontë, Charlotte   24, 25

Browning, Elizabeth Barrett   55

Browning, Robert   22, 40, 55, 60

Bruckberger, Leopold   60

Buchanan, Robert   53

Bulgakov, Mikhail   84

Bunyan, John   58, 77, 78

Burgess, Anthony   47, 53, 83

Butler, Samuel   25

Byron, Lord   40, 60, 78

Caillois, Roger   83

Caine, Hall   23

Calvin, John   50, 58, 63, 69, 70, 76, 77

Camus, Albert   30

Carlyle, Thomas   27

Caswall, Edward   65

Chaucer, Geoffrey   36, 38, 47, 51, 63, 79, 80, 81, 87, 89

Chesterton, G.K.   63

Clark, Glenn   46

Clement of Alexandria, St   72

Clough, A.H.   24

Coleridge, Mary   64

Coloma, Luis   83

Conrad, Joseph   23, 82

Constable, Henry   28

Cony, Carlos Heitor   83

Cowper, William   32, 82

Crane, Hart   61

Crashaw, Richard   21, 28, 31, 39, 58, 76

Csokor, Franz Theodor   83

Cynewulf   50

da Todi, Jacopone   48

Dante Alighieri   31, 36, 48, 51

de Lorris, Guillaume   36

de Meun, Jean   36

De Quincey, Thomas   78

de Voragine, Jacobus   51

Dickens, Charles    55, 66, 70

Dickinson, Emily    87, 88

Dix, William Chatterton    36

Donne, John    21, 36, 59, 69

Doran, Marie    79

Douglas    41

Douglass, Frederick    23

Dryden, John    77

Edwin, Sister Mary    40

Eliot, George    24, 52, 66

Eliot, T.S.    37

Ellison, Harley    29

Epiphanius, St    49

Erasmus, Desiderius    30

Eusebius    75

Evans, Florence    60

Faber, Fredrick William    36

Faulkner, William    23, 45

Federer, Heinrich    83

Fielding, Henry    80

Fitzralph    80

Fogazzaro, Antonio    67

France, Anatole    83

Franzero, Carlo Maria    82

Galdos, B.P.    67

Gaskell, Mrs Elizabeth    79

Gill, Eric    65

Goethe, Johann Wolfgang von    31

Graves, Robert    41, 53, 83

Greene, Graham    44

Gregory the Great, St    49, 57, 79

Grosjean, Jean    83

Gunn, Thomas    55

Hale, Edward Everett    46

Hardy, Thomas    25

Hecht, Anthony    79

Henry, Matthew    69, 70

Herbert, George    27, 39, 48, 59, 64, 77, 80, 87

Herrick, Robert    39, 59

Heyse, Paul    60

Hilarius    54

Hopkins, Gerard Manley    40, 65, 67, 82

Horne, Richard Henry    53

Huxley, Aldous    81

Irenaeus, St    14, 47, 49, 75

Jerome, Jerome K.    46

Jerome, St    47, 49, 51

Johnson, Lionel    63

Jones, David    33, 79

Jonson, Ben    51

Joyce, James    57, 60, 82

Kampf, Harold    44

Kazantzakis, Nicos    53, 60

Keble, John    55

à Kempis, Thomas    20

Kiefer, Warren    82

Kipling, Rudyard    32

Koch, Werner    83

Langland, William    51, 69, 75, 80

Lawrence, D.H.    22, 60

Lernet-Holenia, Alexander    83

Linton, Elizabeth    43, 67

Locke, John    31

Love, Nicholas    48

Ludwig, Emil    41

Luther, Martin    50, 63, 78
Lydgate, John    63
Maeterlinck, Maurice    60
Maier, Paul Luther    82
Mailer, Norman    53
Mandeville, Bernard    51
Marshall, Peter    79
Marvell, Andrew    58
Masters, Edgar Lee    40
McCowan, Archibald    46
Melville, Herman    25, 29, 56
Meredith, George    82
Miller, Arthur    81, 83
Milton, John    21, 31, 36, 42, 43,
    54, 64, 77, 82
Moore, George    53
Moore, Thomas Sturge    53
More, Thomas    28
Morris, William    90
Morrison, Toni    82
Mota, Fernando    60
Nemerov, Howard    71
Newman, John Henry    25, 33,
    65
Nicholson, John    60
Nietzsche, F.W.    22, 57
Noonan, John Ford    55
O'Neill, Eugene    56
O'Sullivan, Vincent    83
Origen    58
Osgood, P.E.    70
Pepler, Hilary D.C.    82
Phipps, William E.    61
Plath, Sylvia    29, 55

Poole, Matthew    27
Pope, Alexander    31, 43, 59, 64
Porter, Peter    82
Quarles, Francis    54
Robinson, Edwin Arlington    56,
    70
Robinson, Thomas    59
Rossetti, Dante Gabriel    65
Rostand, Edmond    88
Ruskin, John    66, 78, 84
Russell, George    53
Ryman, James    27
Sayers, Dorothy L.    41, 47, 60, 85
Schweitzer, A.    42
Scott, Sir Walter    64, 84
Scotus, Sedulius    80
Sedulius, Caelius    39
Seeley, Sir John    22
Sergius, Pope    28
Shakespeare, William    51, 81,
    89
Shaw, George Bernard    59, 60,
    78, 82
Sheldon, Charles    46
Shelley, Percy Bysshe    90
Sienkewicz, Henry    79
Simpson, Louis    61
Sinclair, Upton    46
Smart, Christopher    87
Smith, W. Chalmers    33
Soldati, Mario    83
Southwell, Robert    58, 76
Spenser, Edmund    28, 31, 76,
    81, 87

Stackhouse, Perry J.    70

Stead, William    46

Steele, Sir Richard    43

Steinbeck, John    44

Sterne, Laurence    29

Strauss, David Friedrich    52

Swift, Jonathan    52, 77

Tacitus    75

Tansillo, Luigi    76

Taylor, Edward    87

Tennyson, Alfred, Lord    40, 55, 78, 82

Tertullian    49, 57

Thackeray, William Makepeace    78

Thomas, Dylan    60

Thomas, R. S.    67

Thoreau, Henry David    79

Tillotson, Archbishop    31

Traherne, Thomas    31, 87

Turnbull, Agnes    41

Twain, Mark    56

Vaughan, Henry    31, 69, 87

Vidal, Gore    45

Wager, Lewis    58

Ward, Elizabeth S. Phelps    43, 67

Ward, Mary Augusta    46

Warren, Robert Penn    52

Wells, H.G.    85

West, Morris    79

Whichcote    31

Whittier, John Greenleaf    82

Wilde, Oscar    65, 78, 90

Wilder, Thornton    25, 79

Woolf, Virginia    32

Wordsworth, William    24, 60, 64

Wyclif, John    63, 79, 80

Yeats, W.B.    56